ASK
THE MEDIUM

next door

WITH

Bonnie
Page

*Opening the Window
to the Spirit World*

Bonnie Page

BALBOA.PRESS
A DIVISION OF HAY HOUSE

Balboa Press books may be ordered through booksellers or by contacting:

Balboa Press
A Division of Hay House
1663 Liberty Drive
Bloomington, IN 47403
www.balboapress.com
844-682-1282

Print information available on the last page.

ISBN: 978-1-9822-5750-7 (sc)
ISBN: 978-1-9822-5751-4 (e)

Balboa Press rev. date: 11/04/2020

Seeing Spirit is Special, No Matter How It Happens: Seeing Lucky

Dear Bonnie: I have been seeing spirit out of the corner of my eyes and wondering if this is possible. I usually dream about my loved ones, but seeing while I am awake is starting to get stronger. Can you tell me more about these visions?

We all have the ability to connect to the other side. There are two ways of seeing spirit — objectively and subjectively. Objectively is to see while your eyes are open, and subjectively while you are dreaming or seeing inside your mind through your third eye, located in the middle of your forehead. It is rarer to see spirit with your eyes open, but it does happen. Let me tell you about one of my first times seeing outside of my third eye.

When I was 12, I had a dog named Lucky. He was a small mixed breed, and I had been asking for a dog for a long time until my father gave in and we came home with him. Lucky and I grew together and, being my first dog, we were very connected. He was a very active and free-spirited dog. He would sleep by my bed at night and I always had my hand hanging off the side to be touching him. He also had a box of toys next to him to console his need to chew. He was a very happy dog.

I would always say goodbye as I got on the bus that came to take me to school each day, but this one particular day, I felt rushed as I was late getting started for my day and didn't take the time for our morning goodbyes, thinking I would see him soon. One of my greatest joys was Lucky waiting for me to get home from school, but this day would stay with me through life.

Arriving home from school, I rushed in the house to find Lucky was nowhere to be found and started to call for him when my dad delivered the sad news that Lucky had gotten out the front door and had run out into the road and been struck by a car and had passed away. I was devastated. I cried and felt especially sad having not said goodbye to him that morning. I felt the pain and guilt that maybe he ran out looking for me.

My parents rarely left me alone, but one afternoon, a week after Lucky's passing, they let me stay home as they went to do an errand. Coming out of my bedroom and heading into the living room, next to the fireplace I saw Lucky. I couldn't believe what I was seeing. He was sitting there bright as day with a big smile on his lips and wagging his tail.

He was so happy I could see him. I shouted his name and headed over to pat him, and I almost reached him when he disappeared. I couldn't believe what had just happened. I was so excited to see Lucky with that smile on his face and to see him so happy and very much alive. Our connection, I am sure, made this happen. He needed me to know he was okay even though we no longer could be together in the psychical world.

Heading back into my room, I looked down to see Lucky's toys out of the closet. My mom had put them away so as not to be a reminder, and to my surprise, they were newly chewed with tiny new bites in them, and they were placed all around the room. I couldn't even believe what I was seeing.

I left the toys as they were to show my mom that Lucky had come to visit. My mom, being a medium herself, was amazed that Lucky had such energy that he left proof of his visit. Being a little girl, it didn't take all the pain away, but it surely helped knowing he was safe in heaven and very much alive.

I don't see outside, or objectively, as much as I used to, but it sure is a gift. Now it's more controlled as to looking inside my third eye to see. If you are seeing outside your peripheral vision and seeing signs from spirit, welcome them, and your spirit sightings will get stronger.

Another way of seeing that is very common is in dreams. If they seem real and you can see colors or you find yourself having a conversation with a loved one in heaven, it's a visit — and one you don't want to miss. Keep a journal and a pen next to your bed and write down your visions as soon as you can to remember these precious moments.

Strive to Make Earth a Little More Like Heaven

Dear Bonnie: Do you believe in heaven? And if so, do you think there is also a "bad place"?

I often wonder if Earth is a bad place, and if we are good, we go to heaven. Terrible things seem to happen here that just can't be explained. I did not grow up in a loving family environment, and once I was out on my own, things just never got better for me. Relationships seem to fall apart, and every dream I dare to dream just doesn't happen for me.

I absolutely do believe in heaven, and as a medium, I can assure you it does exist. I know that's easy for me to say since I work with spirit and heaven every day, and as a medium who does this work for healing purposes, I see a lot of hurt in the world and certain circumstances that happen that there are no answers for. I can only tell you what I have been shown and heard from the spirit world.

Early in the beginning of opening up to spirit and using my gifts, spirit would show me in my dream time how beautiful heaven is. I would come into consciousness and become aware of a beautiful field with flowers and grass, skies so blue, colors so much more vivid and bright. I was shown all the animals walking together in pastures that had no fences, animals that here on Earth would be natural enemies, but in heaven were nothing less than loving.

One night, I sat straight up in bed with amazement as they let me hear the music that is being played in heaven, so much more magical than you could imagine. It sounds like a fairy tale, for sure. I feel I am no more special than anyone else, but I am here to teach the things I see and hear so others will know for certain that heaven does exist.

I sometimes now wake to see and listen to myself having complete conversations with those I love on the other side. I don't always remember what we were saying, but I do get to see a little of what's taking place. One night, I even woke up knowing I was in heaven, having a conversation with my mom.

To answer your question about the bad place, I assure you that there is no fiery existence, as has been depicted in the movies. I was shown that this "place" exists only as a collection of your own thoughts and state of mind, and when we pass from this state of consciousness, we bring these thoughts with us to the other side.

In heaven, there are many levels of enlightenment. For example, if you have learned your life lessons and your soul has grown and expanded, you would start at a higher level than someone who has made bad choices for themselves and others. They would start their journey in heaven at a lower level until more light could be brought to them. Light always takes precedence over dark, just like good always conquers evil.

We are all God's children, and He doesn't want to punish us. He wants us to become the most loving version of ourselves that we can be. Earth is our schoolroom, where the lessons are learned. We will never live a life without obstacles to overcome or hard decisions to be made. They are the lessons we need to go through and learn from, allowing our souls the opportunity to learn the unconditional love for others and ourselves.

Your life is all about making choices. Choose wisely for yourself, and Earth might seem a little more like heaven.

Learn What Your Soul Purpose Is and Act On It: Is Your Higher Self Talking to You?

Dear Bonnie: I have so many ideas that float around inside my mind that are good ideas about work or how to make my dreams and plans for my life happen, and I take a mental note to acknowledge them but then get distracted. And then I go on to something new, never putting my thoughts into action. How can I stop doing this? And where are these thoughts and ideas coming from?

Many of us hear thoughts that come and go in our minds. When I was little, I wondered if everyone was always having a conversation with themselves like I seemed to be having. It was like having a friend to talk to. I now know that it is my higher self talking back to me.

What is your higher self? It is the absolute best of you that lives in your soul. We all are souls having a physical experience here on earth, but first and last, you are a soul being. Our soul chooses to come into the physical plane and have an earthly experience to learn many new lessons but also to carry out our soul purpose.

What is your soul purpose? We came into this lifetime for the experience and desire to learn something new or feel and act differently than the last reincarnation, a chance for the soul to expand and grow. We learn new ways of dealing with life.

Your soul purpose is to accept and love yourself and, at the same time, learn how to develop into a better and more understanding person. The soul's purpose usually involves opening up to the realization that we are all one with each other and that we must learn how to help others and humankind.

We are given many chances to become one with our higher selves and realize what love and life are all about and how we can become all that we are meant to be. I believe it starts with self-love and how we feel about ourselves.

That is why we have that little inner voice always asking us to do the very best thing for ourselves and others, that small voice that always tells you the other person's side of the story when you get angry at a friend or family member, the little voice that comes from the absolute best of you that never has a negative thought or feeling, but tries to make you see the true meaning of what is happening around you.

So why are all these thoughts and ideas running around your head, but then you never act upon them? Well, that is up to you to do the work, and your own free will kicking in. We can hear thoughts of help, hope, or creativity, but might never follow up on the ideas.

So if you hear thoughts for you to move ahead on a new job, a new relationship, or a creative idea, they all could lead you to success, but that would take you having that conversation within yourself. My dad used to say you can lead a horse to water, but you cannot make it drink.

If you are receiving guidance from your higher self, try listening and then writing down your ideas. Take even small steps, one at a time, in the direction you wish to see happening in your life. Make sure not to listen to any negative thoughts that pop up, like you're too old to do that or not smart enough or as pretty as someone else, because that's just your ego talking.

No one wants to see you fail, so make a plan and learn to listen to that inner voice that loves you and wants nothing but for you to succeed.

Message from the Divine: Be Kind and Brave

Dear Bonnie: Do you have any messages from the spirit world during this time? I often wonder what heaven is like, and any insight you might have would be much appreciated. Anything to lift my spirits would be great.

I know these are trying times as we are all going through this together. I channeled a message and I am happy to share it with you: "The Magic is within each and every one of you. Have courage as you all will be called upon to give something of yourself. These are difficult times. You have the choice to become stronger in your faith or to resist with the knowledge that we are all near, and not to feel alone when, in reality, you are not. Be kind to each other as this is the key to getting by with love and humanity. Be brave and know deep down in your heart we are praying for you as well. — The Divine"

Last week, I was having a 'poor me' day when I realized it was my sister and her husband's anniversary, and I needed a card. I keep all kinds of cards that I pick up here and there, along with cards that people have given me through the years, together in one place.

As I went to find a card, I was drawn to an envelope that said, "To our baby daughter, Happy Birthday," that was written in my mother's handwriting. My mom and dad are both in the spirit world now, but I had saved that card from five years ago. I loved seeing my mom's writing and how she seemed to put so much love into her cards.

When I looked inside the card, here is what it said on the front: "If there's a mountain in your way, start climbing. If there's a river across your path, plunge in. Believe you can reach your goals, and no obstacle is insurmountable."

My mom had chosen that card years ago, but finding it in a time that I needed to hear from her was amazing. Talk about signs from heaven. Inside was my mom and dad's handwriting, as she always wrote the message and had my dad write "Dad" on the card himself.

Was it fate that I should find this card on the day I needed some reassurance? I would like to think it was my mom directing me from above to find the perfect message I needed to hear on that day and bringing some peace, that I needed to feel their love and encouragement from Heaven.

My insight would be to love each other, do your best, know that we are never alone, and find the courage to accomplish everything your soul has come here to do. Don't let mountains get in your way — climb over them.

Don't Worry — We All See and Hear Things

Dear Bonnie: I have heard voices from another room, someone calling my name, and no one is there. Should I be worried?

We are all born with psychic centers called the clairs: clear-seeing, clear-sensing, and clear-hearing, along with taste and smell. These gifts are what I use as a psychic medium. They are what I use to communicate with the spiritual world.

By the time I was four I was seeing, hearing, and sensing the spiritual world around me. As a child and a grown-up, it can be scary to experience something that you do not understand a lot about or something strange that is starting to happen that has not occurred in the past.

So why now? I have been receiving many emails from people telling me they are experiencing flashing lights (and their eyes are perfect) or knocks on the door, and when they go to open it no one is there, or hearing voices (like yourself), or light bulbs flashing on and off (which happened to me).

I have been seeing many signs that are so strong they make me wonder what is going on, but then I took a moment to think about what is happening in our world and our lives during this pandemic, the most trying of times. I realized the spiritual world, which includes God, Jesus, and the angels, as well as your guides and loved ones, is in high gear and trying to get through to us. We are being watched over and protected on our journey, and when we are stressed or worried, spirit knows our thoughts and tries to send us a message. It might even be in your dream time.

Our psychic centers open to receive this information and may become stronger at different times, and because we all have these gifts, we can receive the signs and information that is going on around us.

Meditation is the number-one way to quiet the mind and open to the spiritual side of life, so if you are hearing, seeing or sensing things more during these times, take the time to engage with spirit.

Find some time in your day to meditate and to ask the questions you would like answered. You might be surprised at the answers you receive when you take that time for yourself and the spiritual world to connect.

How Does One Stay Positive in These Tough Times?

Dear Bonnie: I have been watching your "LIVES" on Facebook, and you seem so cheery even when the world is coming to a standstill. Is there something you know that we do not? Because this is getting tough.

I am going through the same tough times as well. My outlook might be a little different, as I know in my heart it is always better to look forward to good things happening instead of focusing on the things that I cannot change.

I can only do my part to help the world and try not to add to others' pain but to embrace everyone with compassion and love and try to be some sort of inspiration in these darker times.

I heard a saying on television: "Feed your soul." What exactly does this mean? I took it as, what would help you to feel like you were putting your best foot forward at this time with the resources that are available to you?

I can share with you what my family and friends have been doing to bring some food to your soul while helping others at the same time. Here are some examples, and maybe one or two will resonate with you, or you will think of some ways on your own.

Zoom: This is a great way to stay in touch and see the faces you long to see. Before this, I had not used Zoom. I sat and watched YouTube to learn how and then downloaded the app. Not only did I start using it for business (mediumship readings are great on Zoom), but for taking classes as well.

On Easter, my husband's family and I gathered from all different states — some wearing bunny ears — and chatted for well over an hour. It was so nice to see family from Florida and Chicago and here and feel like we were all in the same room. My sister-in-law told us all how she was using Zoom to have lunch with her students once a week. What a great way to give back to children who might be missing the camaraderie of their friends.

Get creative: This is a great time to bring out the paint that has been sitting there because you have wanted to paint a room but haven't had time.

My Facebook friends have been sharing their newly painted and decorated rooms for us all to see. My friend Terry brought out her knitting needles and ordered supplies on the internet and now has a new blanket.

How about cooking and baking? Now is the time to make that recipe you have always wanted to make but is too time-consuming. I, for one, make a homemade cake, with frosting as well, from scratch. Last Christmas I overheard a guest asking if I made the cookies because they looked great! I heard one of our sons say, "No. They're probably store-bought cookies with canned frosting and sprinkles put on the top so they look handmade." I started to laugh because that's exactly what I had done since my schedule was so busy. I made sure to get in touch with that son and to tell him what I had made.

Exercise: Raise the feel-good emotions in your body and, at the same time, burn off extra calories you might be consuming from being in the house and gyms being closed. I used to teach Zumba in the day. So I again used YouTube to bring me to a class and, at the same time, found a Qi-Gong class that I always wanted to try. Where there is a will, there is a way.

Dancing around your kitchen can put a smile on your face and that of anyone who's watching. Whatever it takes to "feed your soul" at this time is a good thing. When adding something positive, you are spreading that energy into the lives of all your family and friends and even those who you have not met. Say a prayer for each other every day that we will all get through this tough time together, and some good will come out of it in many ways.

We are not blind to those who are suffering and in pain, and we keep them in our prayers. Feed your soul and then find a way to help those you can. No act of kindness goes unnoticed in heaven, and many will appreciate your help in these trying times. Remember those great words — "This too shall pass." Until then, you all are in my prayers and thoughts. Keep looking up.

Now is the Time to Look within Your Soul

Dear Bonnie: With all that is going on in our world at this time, are there any messages from the spiritual world that would be comforting at this time? Have you received any guidance or knowledge?

I have been asked this a lot in the past month if I knew if there was some big message coming down from heaven, and I can only share with you my thoughts and my opinions that I have gathered.

When the virus started emerging, and we were told to become aware and start distancing ourselves, I said out loud, "God is giving us a timeout," only to hear the words as they came back to me. "I have not done this. I love my children," He answered back.

I was startled as I listened and then felt terrible for even having the thought that God would ever wish this on us for any reason. I quickly apologized by sending that thought back to heaven and said, "Of course, you would not wish this on us."

I also loved the idea of having a couple of weeks off and staying in my home until I realized I was selfish with not acknowledging that people were dying. It's a sad day for us all, any way you look at it. Did I need a couple of weeks off to give my soul and body a break from the 9-to-5? That could have been a choice I chose for myself without an epidemic going on.

What I have learned these last few weeks is that people have kind and amazing souls and that we are all stronger than we think we are, but most importantly, that everyone in heaven is with us even stronger in our times of need.

Now, I know lots of people were given a heads-up that "we are here" before this started, and that came with hearing and seeing the spirit world more clearly than ever. I have heard from people all over our country, in emails that they have shared with me, their incredible stories of communication with loved ones in dreams or signs from heaven.

I know in my heart and soul that we will never be the same after experiencing this time in our lives. I believe we will never again take for granted the love that permeates in our hearts for our family and friends, and for those we have never met, that we will view all the love and freedom as beautiful connections to humankind and our nation.

Look deep into your soul and ask yourself: "What am I learning from having this experience on Earth at this time? What can I do to help make my family and others feel safe, wanted, and protected?"

I channeled a message from heaven and heard you are loved, and in this time there are two choices: find the faith and compassion within your heart and use that to help others in some way, or get caught up in your head and let fear diminish all you could be doing at this time to help others and yourself. The choice is yours.

Turn inside of yourself and reconnect with your soul, as this is the time for you to see what matters the most to you and your soul's journey. That was the message, short, but sweet and to the point. God gives you free will and does not take that away.

I ask you all to take that in-depth look within yourself to find what your soul was meant to do in this lifetime and to see if you are on the course that was always there before you. You have always had the power.

Living a Life of Gratitude While Looking for the Goodness in Others

Dear Bonnie: I find it hard living in today's society where no one seems happy anymore. The people I encounter don't seem to be interested in anything I have to say or even smiling back if I do make the effort. I want to live a happy life, but it almost seems impossible in today's world. Do you have any suggestions?

I know it seems hard to live a life filled with gratitude, but it does seem to help if you put your best foot forward. We can only take responsibility for our actions and not the actions of others. We can start each day by taking a moment to thank God for the little things as well as the big events that happen in our lives. Living a life of gratitude can be demanding, for sure, but when you make the effort, it does pay off.

Last week, on my cruise to the Caribbean, I took the chance to face one of my fears of riding a horse. I grew up with horses and I do love them but have had some pretty terrifying moments when riding. I decided I was going to try again on an excursion.

The last time I rode was on my pony, Sonny. He was a beautiful, painted pony, but young and had his own ideas. We started on a ride that ended with me being pulled through the woods. As Sonny looked down he gazed into a puddle, saw his own shadow, and became frightened. He bolted with me and off we went.

I managed to bring him to a halt just a few yards away from a huge hole that surely would have swallowed us up. I was only 12, and that was the start of my riding adventures.

Later, as I was riding, the saddle became loose and I ended up underneath the stomach of my pony. Angels were very much with me that day, as Sonny became perfectly still and did not trample me. It's like an angel was holding his reins as I gently fell to the ground.

So on this day when I decided to put these memories to rest, it didn't entirely turn out as I imagined. Almost instantly I became overwhelmed with anxiety as I climbed up on a horse named Ginger. She immediately knew I was hesitant and started misbehaving, putting her head down and bucking. That was enough for me — I wanted off.

Then a guide came around and took the reins, telling me I was okay and that he was going to help me. I had to take a deep breath and ground myself. My guide stayed close, and as we rode along the path I started to connect with my dad in heaven, apologizing for having this fear. He loved his horses and was an avid rider. I saw him in heaven riding his childhood horse, Shaggy. I heard him in my mind, saying, "Just because I like something doesn't mean you have to like it."

A little while later, another guide came strolling up on his painted pinto horse, which looked just like my pony, asking me if I'd like to ride his horse. I thought that was so planned out by spirit that I started to smile. Spirit knows everything, and coming to the end of the ride I felt grateful for my guides' patience and thoughtfulness.

I was also grateful as I got off my horse that day and put my feet back on solid ground. It's the small things in life. I took a moment to thank everyone here and in heaven for watching out for me.

You don't need to go on a cruise to find the good in people. Try to look for the bright light even when it's not so easy to do. God has said to me, "Have no expectations of anyone and be pleasantly surprised by everyone."

So just for today, find the gratitude and feel the love. As you give, you shall receive. Find your soul group by becoming involved in the things you like to do. Find support and happiness by making the decision to appreciate the people who come into your life and accepting them as they are. The rest will follow.

11:11 Could Mean Something Special for You

Dear Bonnie: Recently, I have been seeing the recurring numbers of 11:11. The number seems to be popping out to me wherever I go. Can you give me some direction to who might need to get in touch with me or what these numbers mean?

I have been waking up to the alarm clock showing me 11:11 as well, so I did a little research. Keep in mind that the universe or God might be sending out these numbers, as well as loved ones who have passed, and they can have different meanings to different people. It seems that these numbers, in particular, coincide with what's going on in your thoughts and life at the time they pop up. I'll tell you a little about my story.

One day last week I had gone out and filled the bird feeders, and I came back inside and was staring out the window watching the birds eat when a beautiful cardinal came. Now, I know they are a sign from heaven, so I said, "Hello, Mom," and all of a sudden a light that was not on turned on all by itself.

I am a medium, and these things still excite me, but being a little skeptical, I checked the connection and, sure enough, the plug had to be psychically turned on for that to happen, and it had not been.

I have a clock on my mantle that came from my mom that I inherited years ago that sits there just because it's pretty. It's an old-fashioned clock that you need to wind and set to get going. I have never bothered to do any of that, though I polish it now and then, and I hadn't done that either.

Well, I went to bed that evening and came into consciousness when I heard a voice telling me, "Something special is happening for you in heaven and we are going to play some music for you." I often hear voices in heaven, so I just smiled but opened my eyes to look at the clock, and when I did, 11:11 appeared. Then, out of nowhere, my mom's clock in the living room started to chime.

I jumped out of bed to go see the clock coming to life, chiming, but it didn't stop there. The next night, after being asleep for two hours, I was awakened at the same time, 11:11, but this time my mom's clock was playing a tune. I wouldn't have believed it if I hadn't seen it or heard, but I did, and I was amazed. I called my sister, who explained that my mom often gets in touch with her in the same manner.

Here is what I found out about the numbers 11:11, but there are many different opinions out there on what these numbers mean. So you might need to decide what they mean to you and where they fit in. God or the universe may be trying to send you the message that your thoughts are manifesting in the now. Be careful what you let into your consciousness.

You are a spiritual being having a human experience and are the creator of your own time here on Earth. These numbers are often looked at as angel numbers that give validation that they are close by while watching and guiding you on the path you want to create for yourself.

This is the time to picture big, exciting thoughts about how you can live your life and how you can make a difference to the world for future generations. Angels are God's messengers, and they are who bring to you messages of hope and to align you on your path.

When I first started to see the angels a few years ago, Archangel Metatron and his twin brother came to me with the message that God wanted me for something big, and soon after I started to share my gifts as a medium. These numbers tell you your angels are saying take action now, for it is your time to create the life you choose for yourself.

Stay focused, and if you need to step away from the crowd or your friends for a time to stay in alignment with your purpose, it's okay to do so. Things are manifesting quickly, so be on your toes, expecting only the best for your life. Your dreams are coming to fruition. Your loved ones from heaven can also be telling you they are close by and watching your dreams, as they come offering support and telling you not to be afraid.

Go for it. This is what you have worked hard to achieve. Keep watching and paying attention. It's your time to shine. Something special is happening in heaven. Be ready for it.

Your Gift is a Blessing, Nothing to Be Ashamed About

Dear Bonnie: I have had the gift of seeing spirit from an early age of five, but I learned as I was growing up, and especially when I started school, not to speak about my experiences. I work now in the corporate world, where I don't dare mention anything to do with being mediumistic. My family is on board with me studying and developing my gifts, but I don't think I am ready to let the world know. How do you deal with the naysayers and people who look at you differently?

I was born with this gift as well. Spirituality was nourished, as my mom was a medium, as well as her mom. I thought everyone would be accepting of this gift to see and hear the spirit world. As you know, that's not quite the case.

It's such a shame that some are not as open to accepting that our souls are eternal, and we keep on living, just in a different way.

I am thankful for the mediums who have the television shows and stick their necks out and try to show others how the communication works. I did not do this work fulltime until I heard the voice of God asking me to, and even saying those words can make some people confrontational.

I run a development circle where I have people who also work in the corporate world who cannot let their co-workers know that they are capable of giving a reading, and it's sad because they see people each day who could use their gift and receive a blessing.

In my own extended family, some know what I do but are afraid of speaking about it, so I go with the flow. Surround yourself with like-minded people and maybe even join a development circle so you have an outlet to grow and share your gifts. I am not saying it doesn't hurt my feelings when people think of what I do as taboo, but at the same time, I bring my thoughts and heart back to the ones who receive a blessing by coming for a reading and receiving guidance and love from heaven.

Keep growing with the intention that you are here to serve the spirit world and those here on Earth who are in need of healing. Be proud of who you are, and never shy away from the gifts God has given you. If someone gets under your skin about the subject, try to turn the other cheek. They are just not on the same spiritual path as you.

We are human, so cut yourself some slack when working with others, because it only takes away the peace that is in your heart. Follow your calling, put the blinders on, and stay your course. People are going to find fault somewhere if that's what they are looking to do. Just be you.

Positive Outlook is Key to Achieving Goals: Consistency is Key

Dear Bonnie: I noticed that you are a spiritual life coach, and I was wondering if you could give me some tips on creating a new plan for my life. I feel stuck doing the same thing day in and day out, and it leaves me with the feeling that every year just runs into the next, without a lot of change. I would like to move forward this year with some new goals for myself.

Resolutions can be a good thing if they are not too hard and are attainable. It's when they are so out of reach that they seem daunting that, even with the best of intentions, our commitment to them can go down the drain, leaving us feeling disappointed in ourselves.

The key is to keep a positive outlook in everything you do. Start with a goal with which you can see some results in a measured way so that when you make strides, you can actually see the results and know it's working. That way, you feel motivated to keep moving forward.

Goals can be a good thing to have, especially if you take the time to write them down or even create a vision board, which can be both fun and creative. Using some construction paper and pictures, sit and write your goals down on the board. The vision board shows what you would like to come to fruition in the new year. When you take the time to create this board, you are giving your goals energy, because whatever you give your energy to becomes your reality.

It's giving the universe permission to step in and help. It's almost like saying a prayer — ask and you shall receive. Don't ever be afraid to ask the universe for its help.

A great time to start your vision board is in January at the start of a new year. Create it and hang it up where you can peek at it from time to time to see what's being accomplished and what still needs some more time or energy. The universe only wants what is best for your highest and greatest good, and sometimes it's in God's timing, so be patient.

Be specific about what goals you want to happen. The more specific, the better, so that spirit knows exactly what you have in mind for yourself. Goals can be anything from losing weight to career or to love. Say you want a vacation. Putting up a picture of a beach with palm trees gives you a vision. One step at a time, but with a little help from spirit.

Always try to stay positive, because things in the physical world can be challenging. Your attitude can be a goal-changer. Be a positive role model, not just for yourself but for others around you as well. People will see you as a shining light of positivity, and this energy will be contagious and brought back to you. What you give out, you receive back.

Keep a high vibrational energy by getting enough sleep, eating as many fruits and vegetables as possible, and staying hydrated. Listen to your favorite uplifting music on the way to work. Surround yourself with positive people during the day, the ones who encourage you to be your best.

Everyone has good intentions at the beginning of the year. Try to keep that vibe going through the following months by doing fun projects, leaving time to socialize, or just to relax and be yourself. All spirit wants is for you to live a life filled with joy and laughter and not to be so hard on yourself. If you feel you need support, join a group or take a class with people who have the same goals as you.

Another great way to keep intentions in the new year is to start the day with daily affirmations. You can do this before you get out of bed in the morning or while taking a shower. One I like to use and that I find helpful is saying the following affirmation three times: "Healthy am I, Happy am I, Holy am I, and so it is." It's a great affirmation that I learned a long time ago. You can also make up your own or find another that fits you.

Either way, starting your day with positive, happy thoughts is a great way to begin your day and keep yourself focused on a great new year.

Put Your Blinders on! Don't Let Others' Negativity Seep into Your Dream Time

Dear Bonnie: I was sleeping, and I woke up to the realization that I had one bad dream after another. I have had a lot going on with friends that I work with being kind to my face, but then not so much when they think I can't see or hear them. It's so competitive at my job and there is so much pressure that it's affecting my sleep time. Any advice?

This week, I also found myself paying too much attention to what others are doing with their lives and how successful they all appear to be. I took those thoughts and feelings with me when it was time to go to sleep, only to have them follow me through the night.

Now I know that I have heard the voice of God telling me to put my blinders on and only pay attention to myself and what I am doing, and the reasons I do things as a medium. I am still human, though, and I am sure you, like me, can find yourself wondering when our time is.

Well, let me tell you what happens when you bring fear and worry into your sleep time. Bad dreams can happen, like snakes are chasing me, or I see myself flying over the mountains and fields to stay away from the harshness we all face on Earth. Your dreams might be different, but needless to say, they are not what we want to be dreaming.

This particular night the spirit world stepped in, and I saw the face of my father, who passed two years ago. I can and do see the spiritual world all the time, but this was different. My father's face and the way he was looking at me with his blue eyes was something special. His face was so close to mine, I could see the pores in his skin.

I then heard the words outside of my head telling me, "Don't be fooled!" — kind of like that saying, "All that glitters is not gold." I know my father saw that I was upset and that my feelings were hurt by people who don't care or know me well. I was amazed at the energy it must have taken him to appear so close to me, bringing with him a message to soothe my soul. The spirit world amazes me over and over again, not to mention the love of a parent on the other side.

It's our lesson in life to surround ourselves with people who genuinely care and want the best for us, and to remove those from our lives who don't. It's okay to be picky when it comes to whose energy is affecting your energy. Protect yourself as you surround yourself in God's white light of protection.

Before going to bed make sure you take time to relax or meditate before you try to fall off into sleep. God has told me it's your thoughts that create your dream time. If you want a visit from a loved one during the night, before falling asleep ask for a visit from them that you will remember in the morning.

All that glitters is not gold — don't be fooled! We all are in this together, so shine your light and try not to let others shine their light into your eyes.

Dog's Soul Will Stay a While Before It Embarks

Dear Bonnie: I had to put my husky to sleep after 15 years of her being one of my best friends. I have been mumbling to myself and still talking to her like she is still around. Tonight, my son and I went out to look at the snow moon and to take a picture. We noticed that in every picture we took, there appear to be white and colored round spots or circles that could be orbs. My question is, could my beloved dog show up as an orb?

First of all, I am so sorry for the passing of your fur baby. Our animals are souls and mean just as much as another soul to us, as they should. Animals that have such a strong bond with us are always here to give support to us on our journey called life here in the physical world.

Many dogs and cats, and all kinds of animals, hang around us for a few days after their passing to make sure we will be all right without them. This could be one of the reasons you keep feeling her presence and continue to talk to her.

As I feel her spirit and blend with her, she starts to tell me about the unique love story the two of you had. Not only did you save her, but she truly saved you as well. There were many stories of love, and she especially wants to call attention to when you first met. Yes, I am blending in with the soul of your husky as she sends me thoughts and images from above.

Animal communication is not my specialty, but it is just as easy to talk to a beloved dog as it is to talk to a dad on the other side. She brings me to a scene when you first met, and she looks into your eyes. She instantly knows that she is the one for you; it seems it took you a little longer.

At the beginning of your journey together, and a few times in between, there were some situations that were a little rough on both of you. She tells me going to school and moving were two of these things. I know that as the family grew, so did the love that bound you all together. I see the woman in your life loves her as well, even though there seem to be some obstacles they work out.

She shows me she waits at the door to go on long walks — the longer the better — and she loved the cold and snow. She hated to leave you behind because you feel more like her child, and regrets having to leave you here without her. After all, she knows you are devastated. She hears you as she passes, giving her words of comfort about running free and being pain-free, and wants you to hold the knowledge in your heart that she is once again without pain and jumping fences freely.

Keep looking up into the sky and pay attention to the lights and the orbs, because you asked for her to let you know she was okay in the spirit world, and she is trying to show you that. Although she misses you, she is happy and alive on the other side. Don't be sad, she asks me to tell you, and also to let you know she is still at the front door scratching her nails against the wood to go on a walk with you.

Keep going for walks and take her along. Even though you maybe not be able to see her, you can still sense her presence. She tells me you have a lot to do yet in this lifetime and to keep doing your best, that others depend on you. You have given her the gift of a long and happy life. Your best friend will always be watching, guiding, and protecting you from the other side of life. She tells me you have got this.

So to answer your question: Yes, keep an eye open and watch for her signs, as love is always love, and her love will always be with you.

My Saddest Reading: Use Your Gifts to Help Others

Dear Bonnie: I recently started to give mediumistic readings, and I love helping others as you do with your gift. However, I am finding that the extremely sad readings are taking a toll on me, and I often have a hard time letting those feelings go. Can you offer any advice?

I have been doing mediumistic readings and soul work for some time now, but still, there are always a few that I have a hard time recovering from.

Just a while ago I had a lady, who I will call Karen, call and ask for a phone reading. She told me how she loved reading my columns and how they had helped her in so many ways. I thanked her, she didn't say much more, and we made the appointment.

When the day came for her reading, I did as I always do. I say a prayer before each reading as they are sacred to me. Then I dialed the phone number and Karen's small, quiet voice answered the call. I asked her if she was in a nice, quiet place that she would not be disturbed. She said yes.

I asked her if there was someone special she would like to hear from. She replied, "No, let's just see who comes through for me." I felt some resistance, but I was happy to do that, knowing that sometimes the person you wish to communicate with is not the first to come through. Sometimes it's the strongest personality or the person with the strongest message.

As I closed my eyes for a moment to see who was coming through, I saw a man who began to blend with my energy, and as he came closer and closer, I knew this was a husband coming through. I started to describe how he looked, the color of his hair, what clothes he was wearing, and told Karen how he had passed. I asked Karen if she understood all that I was seeing, and she confirmed that it was her husband.

I also could see a father standing behind her husband. Karen's husband stood by patiently as I gave more evidence until he sent me these thoughts: I love her more today than when I first laid my eyes upon her. I thought those words were the most beautiful words I had heard from spirit. He showed me his wedding ring and said he would honor his vows and never leave his bride.

Karen started to cry, and I didn't assume why. He stated that things were going on in the home, and he wanted her to know there was no pain. I was always taught just to give the words from the spirit world, so I conveyed this to Karen. She proceeded to tell me she had just been put on hospice. She had very much wanted to stay in her home, and she had just been given pain meds.

Her husband showed me three people would be around her bed, and two of them would be her daughters and the third someone with whom she had become close. Karen said she had two daughters and that she and her nurse had become close. She wanted to know who her husband was with and what they were doing, and I proceeded to paint her a picture of her loved ones in heaven.

As the reading was winding down, I saw not only her husband standing beside her bed but Jesus standing with rosary beads in his hand. It was then that Karen told me she had just been given her last rites, and she was indeed Catholic. I took some more time with her, not worrying about the time, and tried to give her a sense of heaven and its beauty and how she would never be alone but would be surrounded by a beautiful white light where her husband would take her hand, and she would not be afraid.

I have never had a reading hurt deep down inside like this one. Karen was ready to go to heaven but had wanted to make sure her husband would be the first person she would see. She loved him with all her heart.

I told her if she needed me, she was welcome to call back at any time, but I knew in my soul that this would be our last conversation. Karen said, "Bonnie, could I tell you one more thing? Can I just tell you I love you?" Tears began to roll down my face as they are now as I write this. I love you, too.

That was one reading that will forever touch my soul. I hope my words helped in some small way to take away the fear of what she was going through. I cried for three days after that reading. So don't ever take for granted the gifts you have to offer the world. They may mean a great deal to someone you have never met.

Take Charge of Your Energy: Give Saging a Try

Dear Bonnie: I have heard of saging my home and myself to clear energy that has become stagnant. I do not know the steps in which this is done. Could you give me some tips on how to do this?

I would love to give you some tips on how to sage your home and yourself. Energy can accumulate on us and in our spaces through the years, and this energy can become stagnant if not released. An old argument that happened years ago could literally still be hanging around! A clearing is easy to do and does not cost a lot of money. In fact, you can do it yourself with the easy directions below. I use these exact steps in my home and on myself.

The tools you will need include sage, either loose or bundled, as a smudging stick, a shell or bowl, a feather, and matches. That's it! Once you've gathered these items, you're all set to go. Any metaphysical store or natural health-food store should have them or you can find them online.

Saging, or smudging, is a cleansing and healing ritual that has been around for thousands of years and comes from Native American culture. The act of burning sage and fanning the smoke around the room with a feather removes the old energy and brings in the new. It's healing on a physical, spiritual, and emotional level and helps rid you and your home of unwanted residue that has been left behind.

Starting on yourself, standing with your smudging stick or your loose sage in a shell, light the end with a match and let it burn for a few seconds before gently blowing the flame out. The resulting smoke is what you want to work with.

Now, starting at the top of your head, say a prayer of intent to remove any energy that is clinging to you. You may call on your ancestors, angels, guides, and great spirit to ask for their help with this ritual. They hear you and are glad to help. Use the feather to gently push the smoke in your direction. Next, you will want to continue in this way, working down the length of your body, legs, and arms.

Visualize the negative and old unwanted energy going down into Mother Earth, where she will send it back up transformed once again. When you have reached your feet, bring the shell back up to the top of your head and fan the smoke to your back and all the way down. Waft the smoke all around you, with you in the center. Give thanks to all.

When you are finished, step away and breathe in love, courage, and a new feeling of strength. Make sure you allow the smoke to stay around you or in your room for a few minutes before opening a window and releasing the smoke. It's the smoke that gathers the energy that was around you or in your room, so we must release that smoke for it to be cleared.

To clear the energy in a room use the same tools, but start in the middle of the room. Now waft the smoke to the four corners of the room, top to bottom, moving around the room in a clockwise manner. Then back out of the room through the doorway and "seal" up the doorway to the room with smoke. Let the smoke sit in the room, grabbing all the old energy for a good five minutes, and then go back in and open a window to let in the fresh air and allow the smoke to leave. Give thanks for all who guide and protect you.

Give this a try and feel the difference in the atmosphere in your space and the lightness in your body. You can follow that ritual by lighting some sweet grass, as it is known to bring in blessings.

In these days of staying home, it cannot hurt to try a ritual that removes old and unwanted energy from your atmosphere and brings a sense of peace.

It's True: All Dogs Go to Heaven

Dear Bonnie: I have heard that all dogs go to heaven. Do you believe this to be true? I just lost my family beagle, and I am so distraught. I would like to believe that our beloved fur children know the way over the Rainbow Bridge, but I would like to know your thoughts.

I know that our beloved pets and animals are never left behind and are treated like the blessed souls that they are. Let me tell you about a personal story that happened to me. It is a hard story to write about, as it has such a tragic ending, but I feel this story will help to heal a lot of hearts by telling it.

My son was in the Army and needed to leave his dog with my husband and me while he went on special duty. His dog became the baby of the family and very much loved by both of us. Zeus was a big dog but always gentle as he laid at my feet while I watched TV, and slept beside my bed at night. Zeus and I became best buddies.

One morning as I got out of bed, I looked to see Zeus sitting up on the floor but with a different kind of expression on his face. I reached over to pat the top of his head, but his expression did not change. I went in to take my shower, thinking it was strange that Zeus did not follow me as I got up to go into the other room. I came out of the shower and continued to my room to get dressed when Zeus became violent and, with his teeth showing, began to lunge full-force toward me.

Instantly, the door between us snapped closed, and I did not remember ever pulling the doorknob (hence angels stepping in, as they can if they need to save a life). I was stunned at the way he wanted to attack me. The commotion awoke my husband, and he was able to take control of Zeus. I had gone into another room and was crying when Zeus again bared his teeth.

My husband got Zeus to the veterinarian and told them the story. My son's sweet dog's mind had snapped. I could not make any sense of it. He was now a threat to others and could not be trusted with any humans. My husband returned home alone.

As I went to sleep that evening, a man appeared to me from the spirit world. He was wearing a lab coat and sat on a desk. He assured me I had done nothing wrong, and unfortunately, this sometimes happens.

The next day I was amazed to see Zeus in spirit, walking up and down the hallway. I knew he was in spirit but he seemed sad, walking with his head down. I could sense the remorse as I called to him, and he came close. I whispered, "I forgive you. It is okay."

I started my day as usual until I received a call from my sister, who also has the gift of clairvoyance. She announced that Zeus was stuck between worlds because he felt he had done something wrong. She told me I needed to sit quietly and send him to the white light.

I had never done anything quite like this, but as I sat and connected to the spirit world, Jesus appeared. He quietly asked me to hand Zeus to him. I saw myself reaching down to pick up Zeus, who was a big dog, but as soon as I picked him up, he turned into a puppy and was handed to Jesus. As soon as he was safely in Jesus' hands, they both were gone. Jesus had come to take Zeus into the light where he belonged.

No soul is ever left behind, and I found out firsthand. I know some of the things I am shown are meant to be shared with others, as I never talk or teach without knowing these things are true.

I still miss Zeus and was so sad to tell my son the news of his beloved pet. But I am happy to say I see him happy and healthy in heaven.

Yes, I believe in the Rainbow Bridge, but I am also glad to know that Jesus takes the time for all those pets that might lose their way of getting there. I hope this story eases the minds of those who love their fur babies as their children.

Can a Loved One Have a Regret? When is a Good Time to Have a Reading?

Dear Bonnie: I was wondering when you think is a good time for a person to have a reading. My father passed, leaving a lot of unanswered questions. Can a loved one in heaven have a regret?

The time to go for a reading can be different for everyone. If a client coming for a reading is not ready to open their heart and listen to the message or is still in a state of deep grief, then the sitting and the message might be a hard one for the medium and the client.

A reading can be a very emotional experience. Just hearing the thoughts and memories that a loved one on the other side is bringing through to the medium can stir so many emotions. Some might be ready to deal with these emotions, and some might need some more time to pass before they are able to receive the communication.

The medium is there not to add words or feelings but to be the go-between for the communicator on the other side and the person coming in for the reading. The medium represents the voice of the spirit world.

That being said, many clients come in with the idea of receiving answers to questions surrounding a person's death or a situation that is happening. Many times a client will get the information they have been seeking, and this will bring them peace of mind. But not always do the loved ones on the other side want to talk about their passing or a situation they know is going to upset you, as they know how it is going to affect you.

Mediums cannot make family members or friends on the other side speak about a subject they do not want to talk about. You must remember your loved one in the spirit world still has the same personality, including dislikes and behaviors. If they were not chatty or didn't like to talk about certain things (funny, because I just realized I have never had someone coming through talking about politics), then the medium might not receive the information you are looking for.

Recently I had a client, and as soon as she sat down her grandmother came through, a delightful lady who gave her so many details and evidence of her life, told her how much she was loved, and left her with many family memories.

The message at the beginning of the reading had many intense emotions and memories for my client, so many that she began to shut down, telling me she did not feel loved by her family, and she started to become emotional. She then wanted to take over the conversation and began to talk about her brother and the problems he was causing her in the family. The sweet grandmother did not want to talk about this subject, and the client became agitated.

If you come to a reading having no expectations of what you think your loved ones in heaven should talk about, then you will be pleasantly surprised. If you're waiting for them to say that one magical word or talk about something in the family that is going on, and you just want them to agree with you, then you could be disappointed, even though the medium has done a fantastic job of bringing the loved one through.

Can our loved ones in heaven have regrets? Yes, of course. Just as we can have these emotions while here on Earth, our loved ones can look back on their life here and see what they could have, or maybe should have, done a little bit better.

Lots of dads come through telling me they wish they would have spent more time with their children, gone out and played ball with their sons, or went to their daughters' dance recitals. They convey to me often that they thought they were doing the right thing working all the time and making money to support their family. They were taught that they were responsible for their family's financial well-being and did not realize they were losing precious time and memories.

You are ready to go for a reading when you're prepared to have a conversation with the person you are missing and to feel their presence around you, but do not require them to reveal certain things that you might think are important and they might not. If a person in the spirit world wants to talk about difficult times and circumstances, they will bring it to the attention of the medium, who can then give you the information.

If you are missing someone from your life who is in heaven and you are open to receiving information that is given to you, you will love sitting in the presence and feeling your loved one around you. It is a magical time when you're in a sitting, and it feels like a natural conversation you might have had over a cup of coffee.

Energy Drainers Really Exist: Choose Who You Let into Your Life

Dear Bonnie: I want to make some changes in my life, and I am not sure how to go about this without ending relationships that seem to drag me down instead of lifting me up. How do I know for sure who should I keep in my life and who should I let go of?

One of my tasks as a spiritual life coach is to help others see who is draining their energy. To make the changes you want, you first need to decide who is bringing your energy down.

Sit down with a pen and paper and make a list of everyone in your life: family, friends, co-workers, etc., and then beside each of their names check off who nurtures your soul and who doesn't. The best way to do this is to feel this within you. Sit with your eyes closed and begin to say each of their names in your mind.

What feelings arise in your heart when you picture their face or say their name? This exercise is the first indicator of who is supporting you on your journey and who is not invested in your future. By doing this exercise, you will begin to sense and feel who is draining your power.

Energy drainers are people who lack their own vitality, so they need or want yours. People sometimes want what you have but don't want to put in the work to get to where you are in life or your job. These are the people that often have their own agenda and are leaning on you to get to where they want to be.

Be aware of those around you who are just trying to get something from you. If someone is gossiping with you, they are most likely gossiping about you, too. They may appear to be sweet and kind while taking your energy and using it as their own.

You want people in your lives who lift you up, not drain you. There are always going to be people who are jealous of what others have, but they don't want to put in the work to have what you have. They might want to be fit, but don't want to go to the gym, or they may want to have a clean, uncluttered home, but don't want to take the time or energy to do this for themselves.

Here are some examples of how you might feel if someone is draining your energy. You might experience sleeplessness, a feeling of fear, negative emotions, uneven emotions, low self-esteem, low confidence, moodiness, or over-sensitivity. It might even affect your diet by craving carbs and sugar as a way of bringing your energy up.

We want to identify the people who have this effect on us and make some changes. Just by seeing someone in your life with a new understanding will set you free to decide who stays in your life or who you choose to spend less time with.

Remember, it's all about our journey and making the best and most well-informed decisions. Sometimes it is about bringing these emotions to the surface and then going from there.

Living our best life starts with who we let in our lives. Everyone who comes into your life is a lesson to be learned or a teacher. It's up to you to decipher who is who.

Encourage Children Who See Spirits

Dear Bonnie: I believe I have a child who can see angels and spirits. My son is always looking into the air and laughing, as he seems to be entertained. Do you believe children can see spirits or loved ones?

I do believe children can see into the spiritual world. Up until the age of seven, children are more connected to heaven, as they have just come from this beautiful place of angels and God. When they start school they begin to work with the left side of the brain and begin to shut off their creative, right-handed side of the brain, the place of creativity and imagination, magic, and wonder. The left side of the brain seems to take precedence when math and science are being taught.

I know, for myself, I was not very good in those subjects but didn't understand why until I learned what each side of the brain is responsible for. Lots of sensitive or psychic children have trouble in this area during their school years.

The word "psychic" comes from the Greek word "psychos," meaning "of the soul." What this means is that as spiritual souls, we can access and receive information that is beyond our physical body and our five senses.

When I was just a young girl, around the age of five, my mother would send me out to play. I grew up in the very rural town of Fitzwilliam, and usually, it was just my mother and me, as we had no neighbors. I had a touch of asthma, and the doctor thought it was a good idea that I get some fresh air every day to build up my lungs. So as my mom watched out the front windows, I would go outside near the front steps and play in the garden. Although my mom wasn't far, I was still a little leery of being outside alone.

Soon I began to look forward to these daily events, as a young girl around the same age as myself started to join me. I didn't ask any questions. I just felt the peace of knowing she was beside me playing in the garden.

She was a cute girl with dark hair and bangs going straight across her forehead. Her face was always glowing and smiling.

She became my best friend, and I no longer felt lonely or alone. I don't know why I never told my mother about this little girl until I was much older, but this little girl turned out to be very special. This little girl was of the spirit world.

The house that I grew up in was a historical one-room schoolhouse that my father purchased for my mom. It even had outside bathrooms, or outhouses as they were called. My dad made rooms in the open schoolhouse and, of course, an inside bathroom. The children's energy remained in the framework, throughout the house, and outside where the children would play.

One day, when I was much older, my sister and I were having a cup of tea when I started to reminisce about my spiritual friend. My sister announced, "She was my friend first," and my mother replied, "Oh, the little girl with the dark hair? She has been here for years." We had all witnessed and been a part of this little girl's life in the spirit side of life.

Do you have a sensitive child? If your child seems to be entertained in his high chair, laughing and cooing while looking up or around, he could be seeing grandparents who have passed or angels.

Is your child highly sensitive or seems to sense how others are feeling or what they are going through? Is your child creative or seems to have an imaginary friend she plays with? Does your child have trouble sleeping without a light on or have vivid dreams? Does she see faces as she is falling asleep?

If your child seems older beyond his years, asking thought-provoking questions or talking about things they couldn't possibly know about, he might be connecting to the spiritual world.

My son, at the age of two, would tell me all about the Civil War and who was coming to visit. If your child has unusual things happening that you don't understand, be supportive, as there is nothing to fear. Highly sensitive children are born with a knowledge of the other side. Read books about psychic children so you will know how to answer their questions, or have a conversation with them about what they are experiencing.

I was born with this gift, and I would still call my mom for reassurance when I needed it. Being a psychic or medium is a gift, but it's always better to know what to do with something so special. Don't push your child's knowledge away but nurture her soul as she continues his or her spiritual journey on this Earth's plane.

Our Pets' Souls are Always Reaching Out to Us

Dear Bonnie: I think my beloved dog Jack is trying to communicate with me from heaven, and I would like to know some ways he might be coming through. Can you give me some tips on what to look for? Jack passed just a few weeks ago, and I was devastated when he became ill. I would feel better if I knew he made it across the Rainbow Bridge.

Our animals, or babies, are souls, and Jack's soul would try to reach out to you in many ways. They want us to know they are happy and at peace with their passing. As when we go on vacation, the first thing we do is to call home to tell our loved ones that we made it to our destination. Our loved ones and fur babies want us to know they are safe and sound.

In the beginning, when they first pass, is when you would receive the most signs that they are trying to get a message to you. During this stage, they know you are sad and distraught, and they want you to know that even though they are not in the physical world, they are still very much with you. After they know you are receiving the messages, their visits will become less often as to let you go through the healing process.

When they come so close to you that you can feel their presence around you, this is the time when they are visiting you and you have a thought about them, and then the tear slips down your face. It's because their soul has come so close to your soul.

Here are some other ways your pets can show their presence:

1. You can hear their paws or their nails on your hardwood floors.
2. If your cat wore a bell on her collar, you might hear the bell.
3. You hear scratching on the back door like they used to do when they wanted to go out.
4. You feel them curled up beside you on the couch or your bed.
5. They leave an impression on the cushion next to you showing you they are there.

6. You see them in your peripheral vision for a second or two.
7. You have a visitation at night in your dreams, and you can feel them with you.

The dream part is my favorite and seems to be the easiest way for your pets to have a visit with you. I know my dogs that are in heaven will come into my dream time and place their nose on my nose. It's always the best hello from heaven.

If you want to have a visit from your loved one or fur baby, ask before you go to sleep that you receive a visit and that you remember having this joyful time, so in the morning you will know for sure it was a true visit.

Your loved ones never leave you and are always by your side, protecting and guiding and still very much watching out for you.

Departed Loved Ones Want Us to Enjoy Life

Dear Bonnie: I try to live a life filled with gratitude and love, but this time of the year is tough for me. My mom passed away three years ago, and it is just not the same during the holidays. I am trying to have the holiday spirit, but even the Christmas music playing in the stores so early in the season is sending me to Grinch land. Any ideas of how to get through the next two months and not turn into the Christmas downer?

This time of year is hard for a lot of people who have lost loved ones. It's hard to pretend to be in the mood or excited about holiday gatherings when it feels like a piece of your heart is missing. Try to remind yourself that even though they are not here on Earth with you and you miss them physically not being here, your loved ones can still be very much a part of the holidays.

Our loved ones in heaven love when we include them in family traditions. Have a special dinner and invite family and friends over. Save a place at the table for your mom by placing a picture of her in her spot, then have everyone go around the table and tell their favorite story or memory of her. There are sure to be tears and a lot of laughter as the memories are shared.

When I am giving a reading to clients, one of the things loved ones like to share with me is their holiday traditions. Some liked to do the cooking and some show me how they decorated the table, or their favorite foods, even showing me their favorite pie. They want you to know they are still watching and caring for you from above.

One night I was getting ready to go to a birthday dinner for a friend, and I bent down to smell some roses that were on my table when I heard my friend's husband speaking to me through thoughts. I quickly picked up a pen and started to write the message down.

Here is what I heard: "Your loved ones are still with you from up above, watching and caring from a place of love. They never leave you — just look up where your eyes will meet full of love. Life goes on, but love never dies, and your loved one will meet you on the other side. Till we meet again know that I am there, protecting and guiding with love that's always there. Your Love."

When I stopped and read the words that were given to me by this special person, the tears spilled down my face as I heard, "Please bring her some roses." You can bet that before arriving at the dinner that night, I stopped and got her a beautiful bouquet of roses and gave her this poem.

I hope this helps you realize that we all have someone we are missing, but your loved ones in heaven want you to celebrate and live life to its fullest. I always ask my clients if the tables were turned would you want to see them happy or sad. I know you would want the ones you are missing to look down and see us enjoying life and taking them along for the ride. When you rejoice, they do as well.

Have a Grateful Heart, and Watch the Blessings Flow

Dear Bonnie: Is there a way to build spiritual growth? Some days I feel more connected to source than other days. When I do feel connected, I know I feel much happier inside and less worried. Do you have any suggestions?

It is hard to be positive and feel close to God and the spirit world all the time, and part of that is because we live in the psychical world where there are jobs to do and bills to pay and lessons to learn. But there are some tips I can pass on that have helped me.

First, I always like to start my morning by saying a little prayer and asking God for his blessings for a healthy, happy, and prosperous day. I feel it sets the tone for my day. Believe it or not, when I get up and start rushing around and forget my little prayer, my day doesn't seem to go as well.

In the shower, you can add to that prayer with an affirmation: "Healthy am I, happy am I, holy am I." Say that three times and end with "and so it is." The water from your shower is taking any old energy off of you and giving you new energy to start your day.

We have an increase in our spiritual growth when we are in alignment with our mind, body, and soul. When we are aligned, our day and life seem to be in harmony, and everything seems to flow in a natural state of ease.

Being grateful for what you have in your life now helps. You can see things in two ways. Your glass can appear to be half empty or half full. There are always two ways of looking at everything that is going on in your life at this moment. I am not saying that the world doesn't look scary out there from time to time; it certainly does if you are growing in one or more areas of your life. Taking chances for growth can be daunting if you are not trusting that the universe has your back.

Before moving on to the next step in your life, be grateful for all the blessings you do have at this moment in time. Don't miss out on the gifts that have been given to you, and try to look at the big picture while also looking back at how far you have come.

When you realize what you have in this moment and don't focus on what you do not have, your heart can be open to receiving the abundance and connection you are searching for. Take the time to sit and reflex on all the positives that are going on in your life. Sometimes we are waiting for that one thing we hope comes to fruition, and we miss all the joyous situations and love that are already surrounding us.

Have a grateful heart, and watch the blessings start to pour into your life. Be open to all that God and the angels want for you, and be open to receiving them. Start writing down the blessings that are coming your way each day. It only takes five minutes of your lunchtime to make a list. Don't leave out the small stuff, as they are blessings also. Your dog waiting at the door each night with a kiss for you might seem like a small blessing, but those blessings add up to a fulfilling life.

To be in alignment with God and your heart, nurture your mind, body, and soul. Choose to have a positive attitude, a grateful heart, and loving thoughts throughout your day. Look after your psychical body by what you are feeding it. Take great care of your soul by doing something spiritual every day.

This is your life — make it a good one. Don't get caught up in what everyone else is doing. Focus on what is important to you and stay in the moment. Have a vision for your life, but don't rush your life trying to get there. Your blessings will come to you if you do your part.

Know that everyone up above is rooting and praying for you to have the life you want and dream about.

Have a Grateful Heart, and Watch the Blessings Flow

Dear Bonnie: My friends and I want to go for a reading, but we are not sure if we want a reading by a psychic or a medium. Can you tell me the difference between the two and what they offer?

When going for a reading, it all depends on what you are looking for. All mediums are also psychic, as they can receive and perceive information, but not all psychics are mediums. If you are looking for guidance in your life or on your soul's journey, a psychic or psychic medium would be for you.

Here are some of the questions you could ask the psychic so he or she may focus on a situation for you.

- Is my love life going to improve?
- Do you see marriage and children in my life?
- Is my career going in the right direction?
- Am I on my soul's journey?
- Are there going to be any significant changes coming up?
- Is there anything you can see to help me on my path?

These are psychic questions, but please choose wisely when you are planning who to see. Make sure the psychic is reputable and doing this work for the right reasons. During this time of the year, people tend to come out of nowhere because of the season.

Also, keep in mind that a psychic can see what is going on at the time of your visit, but nothing is written in stone. We all have God's free will, and we all have the ability to change our minds, as does another person in the scenario. Lots of clients come in to see if their boyfriend is the one, but he also has the opportunity at a later time to change his mind about the relationship, hence changing the outcome of the reading.

A medium has the ability not only to read the energy around you or listen to the divine but to expand that gift. They can reach loved ones or animals that have passed, and guides to bring to you a sense of peace that can fill your heart with the knowledge that you are never alone.

All mediums are not the same. Find a medium with a good reputation and one with whom you can relate. I talk about God, Jesus, and the angels, and do this work for healing purposes only. I let clients know this is how and why I do this work, and if that relates to them, perfect.

A medium should be able to sit with you and sense, feel, see, and hear your loved ones who wish to connect with you. I ask who someone wishes to communicate with and write the name and relationship down on a piece of paper before I start to work. It is highly useful but not always necessary.

During the session, I always start with a prayer and then become aware as I see a person or group who are in spirit coming to your session. As I describe the first person stepping forward, I will give many details of how that person looked, relationship to you, age of passing, what took them from here, giving evidence so you know exactly with whom I am speaking.

The second part of a reading is sharing with you the memories of the relationship the two of you shared, events only you would know about, and evidence that you can recall. I always end the reading by asking the person who has shown up for you what they would like to say from their heart to you. It's always the most emotional and heartfelt part of the reading.

Before ending, I like them to tell me a sign that they have been sending to you to let you know they are close, and I also ask them to show me their version of heaven, so you know in your heart who they are with and what they are doing in their time in heaven. Most times, they will also give me information of what you have been doing recently, so you know they are by your side.

A reading can be emotional and have lots of tears, but it is in those tears that the healing can begin to take place in your heart and help you in some small way to move on, knowing your loved ones are still very much around you.

Let's Not Forget the Real Reason to Celebrate Christmas

Dear Bonnie: I want to feel happy and see all the joy that the Christmas season brings, but I seem to feel anxious about all of the pressure of the season and the holidays. I have all these expectations of my family getting along and sitting around the table enjoying a meal together and sharing stories from the past. Maybe it's too much to expect, but it just leaves me feeling empty and wishing my family were like the ones on TV. Any suggestions for having a more peaceful holiday?

I think a lot of us put pressure on ourselves and our families this time of year, but I think it's up to us to remember what the season is all about.

I was in the middle of a meditation a few years back when I asked spirit to show me how they celebrate Christmas in heaven when I heard a big voice telling me, "It's Jesus' birthday!" That statement made it so clear to me that what I focus on during the holidays might not be in alignment with what's going on in heaven.

I always go to church on Christmas Eve and I sing all the songs, but then life here on Earth kicks in, and I start to get worried about presents and the perfect family party or meal. God once put the thought in my head, "Have little expectations with everything and be pleasingly surprised with everyone." That's how I try to live my life.

If you are doing your best and living every day to its fullest and not imagining everything to be perfect every day, it takes all the pressure off and lets in only the enjoyment of sharing the holidays with family and friends while remembering that Christmas is about the birth of Jesus.

If you can imagine Christmas in heaven, celebrating Jesus' birthday and all the angels singing, be at peace with the knowledge that we all are doing our best and we are not meant to be perfect. We are perfect in God's eyes, and He wants all his children to live a happy fulfilling life.

When you're worried, you are not trusting God.

Don't let yourself get caught up in the material or emotional things you think you need to have for that perfect holiday. Instead, go deep within your heart and find the peace that resides within you. If you are looking at others and imagining that their life is so much better, you're not focusing on the joy in your life. If you are feeling lonely or looking for others to bring you joy, giving back to others is a great place to start finding the joy within yourself.

No two families or situations are alike. A great way to find that joy is to give to a family less fortunate than you or to reach out to an animal shelter that could use a helping hand. There are lots of ways to focus on the real joys of the holidays instead of what we think we need to be happy.

Focus on what's truly important and not on artificial things in life. Love is always the best and most important emotion.

Tips on How to Talk to a Loved One Who Has Passed

Dear Bonnie: Do you have some tips for connecting to our loved ones? It's great to see a medium that you know can do this for you, but I would like to communicate on my own and more frequently.

Yes, it truly is possible to connect with your loved ones who have passed to the higher side of life. It sometimes takes patience and a little time, but you can build a strong conversation with the ones you have been missing. No special abilities are required to start the conversation. Start with the intention that this communion can happen and the mindset that it is possible to talk to your loved ones.

Here are some tips.

1. Everything starts with meditation or clearing your mind of earthly chatter to make room for those you love to come through to you. Find a quiet place where you will not be disturbed. Place your favorite picture of the person with whom you wish to communicate, one that brings a memory to mind, in front of you. Light a candle and place it next to the picture.

2. Closing your eyes, begin to take some deep breaths in through your nose and out through your mouth, releasing everything you no longer need or want to hold on to. Do this a few times until you feel yourself becoming relaxed.

3. Soon, the chatter will start to fade away, and you will feel a peacefulness. Start to picture the person in your mind while setting the intention that you're inviting them in. You are calling them with the intention to communicate, and just by thinking this in your mind, you are setting the stage for the conversation to begin.

4. Send out thoughts of love, and give them permission to come forward. If they think they are going to upset you, they will send love but will back away, not wanting to cause you any pain. They know when you are ready.

5. Patience is the key to receiving a message. You might see them in your mind's eye, hear a thought inside your head, or feel them physically as they draw near. Try not to become anxious. When you know they are joining you, I always like to start by saying hello. Open a conversation by asking them a question and then waiting for an answer. You might receive the answer in several ways. Go with your gut feeling. Don't try to make the conversation go in any direction; be open to receiving. When you know they have drawn near, that is the time to let the conversation happen naturally.

6. Be open to receiving your answer when the time is right. This exercise might take some practice and time, but it will be well worth it when you know you can create this scenario, knowing that your loved one is joining you.

Building your psychic ability can take time, but time is irrelevant in heaven, so your loved ones are always happy to communicate with you.

We All Have the Ability, but One Must Exercise It

Dear Bonnie: How do you know if you were meant to be a psychic or a medium? Does it start when you are little, or can you develop the strengths at different ages? I recently had a friend pass two months ago. I have been getting signs I know are from her, and my dreams have been vivid and almost real. Can she be opening my psychic vision?

Everyone is born with psychic abilities. Our five senses all play a role in our abilities, as well as our sixth sense, which is your intuition. All these abilities can become stronger with practice and by knowing that each one is like a muscle that we can build and make stronger with a little practice and discipline.

It's almost like going to the gym where you would lift weights and do biceps curls. Your biceps would start to show and you would become stronger. Same idea with our psychic senses.

Like anything, with time and discipline we all can use our psychic gifts. Say you want to start using a simple method of building up your gut feelings and your knowing ability. There is a tool you can use to start today. Take all the individual ring tones you have for your friends and family off your phone. When you hear it ringing, start by asking yourself internally who is calling and then answer the phone to see if you guessed correctly.

Make sure you give yourself a moment to feel, see, or hear the answer coming to you. If you heard the answer inside your head, you used your clairaudients (your psychic ears). If you saw a picture with the face of the person who was calling, that was using your clairvoyance (your third eye). If you just knew, with no explanation, who was calling, that was your clairsentience (that gut feeling).

The "clairs" are your psychic centers — the centers you can use to build your psychic abilities.

A medium is a person who can bring information from the spirit world to someone here on Earth. The medium is just the middleman, a vessel used for someone to be in service and help others. Most mediums, including myself, can remember seeing or hearing the spirit world by the age of four. The gift of mediumship can be handed down through the generations. Mine came down through four generations on my mother's side of the family.

Sometimes the passing of someone close can also open the third eye (the window to the other side). I am not sure why this happens, except that the loved one in heaven needs to get a message to you or needs you to be the messenger to bring forth a message to one of their loved ones. If you find yourself a sensitive person, the abilities seem to come easier.

One day, as I was working on a client during a reiki session, her husband from spirit started talking to me. He somehow knew I had gotten my feelings hurt the day before and that, being sensitive, I was still hanging onto it. Her husband came into my view, gave me a bright smile, and conveyed the thought to me, "If you were not sensitive, you would not be able to do this work. So next time you get your feelings hurt, say thank you." He made me smile. Knowing that someone I didn't even know here on the Earth plane cared enough to give me advice made me smile and let go of what was bothering me.

If you are getting signs from someone who has passed into the higher side of life, honor them by acknowledging that you are receiving the signs, and you will continue to get more. It is like having a conversation: When you talk back and they know you are receiving, the conversation can continue to take place.

Some are better at remembering visits, but we all have them. Your loved ones never leave your side and always want us to know they are still here with us, guiding us and living very much right beside us. Start building your psychic senses today so the conversation becomes clearer and their guidance and wisdom become stronger.

Soul Searching Leads to Soul Lessons

Dear Bonnie: Do you believe we have soul lessons? Are these predetermined, and if so, can we make choices so the lessons are easily received? It seems some of the lessons that have been showing up in my life are hard to handle.

We are a soul having a human experience. I heard this statement from my years of training in the metaphysical world, but I don't think I truly knew what that meant until one night while sleeping, I was shown how our souls look on the other side.

Before an event one night, I was shown souls waiting in line in heaven to be at the event the next evening and waiting patiently for me to deliver messages to their loved ones. When I see clairvoyantly in my third eye, I always see loved ones who look just like they did while they were here on Earth, but this one night they wanted me to see them as souls.

So to my surprise, I could see bright, beautiful lights with what seemed to be frames of bodies. I didn't see clothing or faces and details of people, as I usually see, just these beautiful souls letting me know they were not going to let me down, they would be there for the show. Although I loved being shown this beautiful sight, I sent a thought to the spirit world: I love seeing you as you were here in the physical world. Since then, that's how I see everyone in heaven.

We are souls that come down from heaven with the intention of learning the lessons that we have decided, along with our guides and masters, would enhance and grow our souls and create a learning experience.

The exact way these lessons are to be learned is not told to us, or we would wait for these lessons to unfold, taking away the opportunity for growth. Life is just our schoolroom or classroom where the lessons can be learned from trials and obstacles that seem to be getting in our way.

Many wonder why this is happening to them. Depending on how you view each situation that comes into your life, lessons may seem daunting and draining. Taking a look at each difficult experience with the knowledge that there is a lesson that can be a teaching opportunity, and looking at each problematic situation in this way, can take away some of the anxiety that might come from having the problem.

See each situation that seems challenging as a learning tool, and ask yourself what you can learn from this experience. Lessons are in our lives to help, not hurt us. So if we can embrace each day and try to understand to take each day as an opportunity to add to our soul's growth, instead of seeing events as challenges, life seems to run a little smoother.

Recognize and acknowledge the lesson and then say thank you and let it go with grace. Only then can the lesson go away.

Tips for Finding the Key to Living a Spiritual Life

Dear Bonnie: I would like to find the key to living a spiritual life. Life can be a bumpy road. I don't think it's meant to be this hard. Any suggestions?

Life can be challenging even for the most spiritual people, but there are a few ways to lift your vibration or raise your energy, and that can make your road seem a little happier and more fulfilling.

Raising your vibration is a way of bringing your energy to a higher level, and in turn, becoming closer to source, creator, and the heavens. This feeling of being connected brings us to a higher level of peace within us. When trouble does rear its ugly head — and it will, because life is our schoolroom and we are here to learn the lessons our soul needs to grow and expand — you will be better equipped to handle difficult situations.

Tip No. 1: Try to be happy at this time and in your current situation. So many people think if only I could be happier. Try to see the happiness that surrounds you currently while recognizing the good in your life today. Start by seeing the joy in even the small things that a day can bring: a puppy greeting you at the door as you arrive home from work, a special friend in your life who is a good listener, your family that supports you.

See the good that surrounds you, and by acknowledging it the rough times seem to get smaller in comparison. If you need to get a journal at the beginning to write all the joys you encounter, that can be a helpful tool. At the end of the day, as you look down at your journal, you will become more aware of the blessings in your life in the here and now.

Tip No. 2: Don't wait until you hear yourself saying, "I will be happier when …," because life is too precious to be waiting for something great to happen to us. Take some time to write in your journal your definition of happiness. Happiness can mean a lot of different things to people. When you write down what happiness means to you, it opens the door to understanding exactly what you would like in your life.

Tip No. 3: Pursue a life of meaning: Find what you are passionate about and work toward helping others with your gift, whatever it may be.

If you're passionate about helping children, find some ways you could be of service. By giving back, you'll find yourself happier, too.

People who live a life helping others and who are not just seeking pleasure seem to be the happiest. Sometimes we need to work at creating joy in our lives. Make the effort to do more joyful things this week, and when you do, write the events down in your journal, and write next to them how they made you feel.

Bring more happiness into your life by surrounding yourself with happy, supportive people and finding joy in the small things. Living a life of gratitude will bring your thoughts to a higher level, therefore raising your vibration to where you will feel more connected to your spiritual self, bringing more happiness and love to you here on earth.

Bad Spirits in Heaven? Well, Then it Wouldn't be Heaven

Dear Bonnie: Do you believe there is a bad place or bad spirits in heaven? You always talk about the good stuff, but I am wondering if that is because you leave the rest out.

Indeed, I would much rather talk about light and love rather than dark, which there surely is.

When I was a little girl, my mom, who was very spiritual, used to look at me when I was being not so nice and maybe a little cranky, and she would tell me, "There is an angel on your left shoulder and the devil on your right shoulder, and you had better knock him off." She would watch me as I laughed, which took away the crankiness and pretended to knock the devil off my right shoulder.

You see, there is always a choice when it comes to every decision we make in life. Being a medium, I choose to do my work only in the white light of God. I have seen things in the spirit world that have scared the pants off me, but knowing in my heart that good always outweighs the bad, the second I think of God, they go poof. Truly, anything that was there disappears.

I believe that as souls living in this lifetime, we all have choices in our lives that are made out of love or fear. It's that basic. There is always a good choice or a bad direction. There is, and always will be, two sides to every coin: love vs. fear, angel vs. devil, trust vs. worry, glory vs. shame, truth vs. falsehood, light vs. darkness.

The choice is yours. We all have God's free will, and that means no one can make our decisions for us. In the spiritual world, they can shine a light to show us the way. They can manipulate changes so that we may see. But in the end, it's all on us and the choices we make. Everyone will face choices they need to make that will push boundaries in their beliefs at one time or another, but if you have love, trust, and truth in your heart, the choices get easier to make.

Are their bad spirits in heaven? No, or it wouldn't be heaven. That doesn't mean they don't exist. I do believe there are different levels of heaven, meaning someone very enlightened who has lived many soul lives might start at a higher level than someone who still needs to grow. Bad spirits don't want to hang out with people who are of the light. It's like a teetotaler who might never want to go hang out in a bar.

At the end of the day, it's about making a choice. Do I want to hang out with the good guys or take a chance getting to know the bad guys? For me, that's a no to the latter. There will always be good vs. evil, and it will always be your choice. Make each decision by asking, "Will this bring me to the light where I may find peace?" If the answer is yes, go with that decision.

Remember my mom's analogy. The angel is on your left shoulder, the devil on your right. Which one do you want to knock off? I sure do love my angels.

Don't Be Creeped Out —
It's Just Your Third Eye

Dear Bonnie: I am new to meditation. I meditated a couple of times and a saw a big eye, like Snuffleupagus, the dog from Sesame Street. Super-big eyelashes. It creeped me out, so I stopped. What was I seeing?

You were seeing your third eye. Your third eye is the seat of clear seeing called clairvoyance. When you are meditating, you are clearing the mind and making room for the divine to communicate with you.

I can remember the first time I saw mine. It was years ago. I remember closing my eyes to sleep, and an eye appeared. It was not scary to me, but I, too, saw the eyelashes, and I actually said, "You're a pretty eye." A voice came in my head and said, "That's your eye."

Since then, I have learned so much about my third eye and how it works. Your third eye is located between the brows in the middle of your forehead. To see internally (your third eye center) is called subjective clairvoyance, which is how a lot of psychics and mediums see to bring forth information from the spirit world.

Practicing opening your third eye is vital when you want to be open to receive information. Meditation is the number-one way to quiet the mind and bring your attention. While focusing on the spot between the brows, with your eyes closed, ask in your mind for your third eye to open and wait patiently, as this sometimes takes time and practice.

Once you see your third eye for the first time, it should get easier to see it open when you request it. Your third eye could be oval and placed to one side, and, yes, it does have eyelashes. You might see just a bright white light coming through at first or even colors. Be diligent in working to become one with your third eye.

Once you do, you are on your way to working clairvoyantly with the spirit world. You may psychically see a person, loved ones, visions of the past, present, future, and people or places in other dimensions. I see photographs when I am connecting to someone's loved one during a reading. This enables me to give an accurate description of the person coming through to connect.

If I take a good look at the person in the photograph, I can see their features, how they are dressed, where the picture was taken, and many more details that give my clients evidential proof that their loved one is coming through for them. The view in your mind could be like a still picture or a movie playing in your mind.

When the image is of psychic origin, the picture will come first and then the thought second. That's when you will know information is being given to you and that you're not trying to make it happen.

Don't be afraid of seeing your third eye. It's one of your psychic senses that God has blessed you with to make your journey here a little easier and a lot less scary.

Medium Should Be a Conduit Between You and Loved Ones

Dear Bonnie: I was wondering about the differences there can be in the many mediums who are now popular and can be seen on social media advertising live events and readings.

I can only speak for myself, but there seem to be more mediums putting themselves out there and drawing recognition to themselves in the hope of giving hope to many. I believe the world needs to feel like there is more to this life than just an ending.

I had a client who came in last week and stated, "I just want to know we just don't go poof and that's it." I assured her we do not just go poof. But how can you be sure about that when your faith has been challenged and you are feeling alone?

Life here on Earth can have many disappointments, and if you are not feeling connected to your higher self or creator, God, or the universe, you might end up feeling very alone. This can happen if you're not sure of what to do to get back on track with that feeling of contentment and knowing that you do have a purpose in this lifetime. You become detached from life.

I feel everyone should experience seeing a connection to the other side. That's what a medium does, especially during an event, is show you how the link can happen in a large gathering. If you are interested but have a fear of having a private reading, an event is the place to go and watch a medium work.

Everyone has a different style of presenting the spirit world to his or her audience, and you might connect to one medium more than another. I know I have my favorite mediums who I like to watch as they work with the other side and how they present the spirit world. I always tell my clients I am the gentlest medium you can find. It's more like sitting down with your friend having a cup of tea.

My television show on Leominster public-access TV is called The Medium Next Door because I wanted to take away the scary idea of having a reading and replace it with the feeling of "Wow! That was a blessing!"

I have had many clients write on social media that they have just had a reading with me, and it was like talking to their loved one as if they were sitting next to them. That's what a medium is for, being the conduit and middleman who can bring your loved one to you for a conversation that you need and want. What could be more precious than that? The experience is priceless to many.

I know firsthand how it feels to live a life on Earth without your parents here. This past weekend, my first grandchild was born, and even though I know my parents were watching and rejoicing with the rest of the family, there still was a hole in my heart as their physical presence was not there.

A medium's job is to give you evidence that your loved one is still here with you but to also convey the message of love that we all miss from them not being here, like proof that they know about the amazing moments we are having since they left us.

Lots of people ask if mediums can speak to our loved ones on the other side. Believe it or not, we do not have access to them at all times. We watch for signs, like songs on the radio or a scent of grandma's perfume. Sometimes, though, I do hear their voice in my thoughts when I need a little encouragement. If we did always have access to our loved ones, we would not live our lives as fully down here as we should. But we need to know we will all be together again one day.

If you have the chance to have a private reading or to go to an event with a medium who is courageous enough to stand up in front of a large group of people and show you the art of communication, what could it hurt to take a chance? Attend with an open heart and mind, and ask spirit to guide you to the right medium for you.

We all work a little differently. I try to bring in some lightheartedness to ease the fear people may have while at the same time showing compassion and giving evidence, so there is no doubt of who is coming through to you during a reading.

In the end, it's all in how you want to perceive the experience. For myself, it's a blessing every time I bring a loved one close enough that you can almost feel them. I know that's how I like to feel when a colleague brings through one of my loved ones to me.

You Only Get One Soul — Make Sure to Use it Wisely

Dear Bonnie: I used to feel so happy, and as I have grown older life seems to have kicked me in the butt. How do I get back to a place of feeling connected to God and spirit and start to feel grounded again?

One thing we need to do as we go through life is to make sure we don't let the troubles of the world weigh us down to a point of losing or dimming our inner light. Your inner light is a gift to you that is meant to shine bright. We are born with this light inside of us when we come into the world.

You can close your eyes and bring yourself back to a simpler time around the age of five or six and picture yourself standing in a field of flowers or inside your family home. See that little girl or boy with that smile upon your face knowing that you are connected and safe, your innocent soul not yet aware of the things of Earth that are hard, like feeling the pressure of earning a living or making sure dinner is on the table or even the feeling of not being enough or having enough. Embrace the childlike existence of just wanting to be loved and cared for and full of joy as you play.

Life can seem to burn out that shining light of hope and fearlessness we have when we are born. The soul comes to Earth with a purpose for this lifetime. We feel fulfilled when we are on that path, but if we have strayed, either by giving up a dream because it seemed frivolous to the world or our parents, or because the opportunities didn't appear for us, we might forget why we are here on this journey called life.

We bend our dreams so they fit into a box of what we think we are supposed to be doing and forget the childlike instinct to enjoy the now and look for the fun. We ignore that gut feeling of taking classes in school that we might enjoy and excel in because they might not get us the job that makes a certain amount of money, and we have a fear of not meeting others' standards.

When we come from a place of fear and not love, we are ignoring our inner light. We replace it with a what-if. We have two choices in life: We can be fear-based or love-based. Those are the only two choices, love or fear. Our ego tries to keep us safe by becoming fear-based, but limits how high we can fly and our ability to bring our dreams to fruition. Love can be scary at times, but so worth the chance of happiness.

If you take a chance and it doesn't work in your favor, at least you tried. Keep trying until you get that promotion, job, or relationship you have been searching for. You are meant to have a fulfilling life full of joy.

My advice is to shine your light as brightly as you can, let go of fear and ask yourself what your six-year-old self would want. We are only here for a short time. Why not live with the enthusiasm of our young soul that has so many plans and dreams?

Always come from a place of love, not fear. Take care of your soul — you only have one.

Can She Ever Find Another Soulmate?

Dear Bonnie: I recently broke up with my boyfriend. He says we are soulmates and he wants to continue the relationship, but I believe the relationship has run its course. If he is my soulmate, does that mean I won't find someone new?

I believe we have many soulmates and even a soul family. We come down to Earth each time we reincarnate with our soul family so that we can teach and learn valuable lessons.

In our new-age way of thinking, if you have met your soulmate, everything should be perfect, and we are meant to be together forever. That sounds like a fairy tale to me, but it does sound nice.

The truth is that each person in our life is here to teach us a lesson our soul needs to learn to grow and expand, becoming more enlightened each time. When this lesson is learned, the relationship could move on or change when the mission is accomplished. Some relationships are meant to last a lifetime while others just a short time.

Each relationship we have offers something new and challenging. Think back to the time you first met your boyfriend. What drew you to him? There was an attraction for a reason, something that made your heart swell and made you know you were meant to be with this person.

Ask yourself what this person has taught you since you committed to being in this relationship. If it seems the lessons have been learned and the spark has seemed to have fizzled, maybe both of you have done your part. It's a good idea before leaving any relationship to look at the big picture and view each side.

It is not possible to go through life without having a few bruises and bumps along the way. Here is an exercise that would help both of you to move on with love and compassion, which is a lesson of its own.

In each relationship in our lives, cords of energy can be attached to each person. Cords are not always negative energy but can be from those we love. Cutting these cords and sending them back can free your own emotions and help the other person as well to feel whole and loved without clinging to your energy.

Try this: Sitting back in a comfortable chair, holding onto a piece of rose quartz crystal (the crystal related to the heart chakra), sit with soft music playing, and begin to feel yourself becoming relaxed. Call in your guardian angel and ask him or her to give you a sign that he or she is nearby, feeling yourself receiving a gentle hug. Feel the love and affection the angel has for you.

Now, going down to the center of your chest to your heart, feel your heart beginning to fill with love. Send healing energy to your heart and picture a pink ball of light shining brightly. Now picture the person who has hurt your feelings or wounded your heart, someone you would like to release from your energy field.

Allow the healing energy to go to the person you are seeing in your mind's eye. See the connection between the two of you. See the cords that have attached between you. These cords can look and feel very different: some lighter, some darker, some thicker, or some appearing thin like spaghetti.

Ask your guardian angel to remove any painful cords, leaving only the love you feel for each other. Ask that any lasting emotions or thoughts be taken up to heaven and the higher side of life. Give yourself some time to do this. Ask the angels to help you move forward in your life and to see only the best in the person you are leaving or have an attachment to.

Be free to love again and live each day with love and compassion and to have a heart that is filled with love for yourself and others. We are meant to live a joyous life filled with love.

We Choose Our Own Paths, Even When to End It

Dear Bonnie: I want to know why everyone who means the most to me has passed away so young. Please tell me what I can do to change my life with a positive outcome.

I am genuinely sorry to hear of the ones you love passing so young to the higher side of life. Before we came to Earth, our soul family (those who reincarnate with us again and again in many lifetimes) sat down with the masters and guides and decided what each one of us wanted to learn this time around in order to experience different circumstances that would let our souls expand and grow.

There is a blueprint of our lives, a plan of experiences and circumstances that we want to experience, but indeed not the choices we make, for each one of us has free will. If we didn't, we might be happier with everything always going our way, but there would be no lessons to be learned, and we might all look and act as puppets, which is not intended for us.

Each soul comes here with the knowledge that life here will be difficult, with many lessons to be learned as a way of letting our soul expand and grow. When we accept the trials and tribulations that are given to us, and they are not just endured, we come to realize there is a lesson in everything that happens in this lifetime.

Love is the reason for our existence, and by learning to love with an unconditional love that has no prejudice, and knowing that everything is just as it is supposed to be, we live with the knowledge that each lesson is meant as a way to personal growth.

Your soul family that came here this time with you may have decided they did not want to live long lives, or their free will of life choices could have hurried them back to heaven sooner than expected. Without the full knowledge of each situation, I can only assume you are here to learn lessons that you have chosen for yourself.

A young life going back home could be that person's choice, or the lesson might be yours to learn. I am sure that with each passing, you had to learn to be stronger without the person you depended on and assumed would be here with you much longer. Sympathy and compassion reflect the growth of your soul, as each passing brought about these two things. It is not easy living in a world where everything is not a given, but only a blessing, and sometimes just for a short while.

I know it's not always easy to see the bright side of things, but if you strive to live a life trusting the process and having faith in your heart, living this time on Earth might be a little easier. Face every day as a new beginning and try to see the beauty in every new blessing and pain, knowing that each situation is a chance to see your soul's growth.

When we start to embrace and not fear our journey, the change in our attitudes can be amazing. Trust in God and have faith believing that there is a plan and that we are being guided and loved from above, knowing we will see and be with those who love us once again.

Divine Ways to Lose Weight and Achieve Other Goals

Dear Bonnie: Do you think the Divine helps you with all things, even losing weight? I was at a summer barbecue where the focus turned to losing weight and why it seems to be so hard for some. I felt the frustration of some living in their body. Is there a way for a Divine intervention?

I genuinely do believe that the Divine wants everyone to be living their best life. Every aspect of what we are going through in our lives is important in the spiritual world. When we are not happy with how we look and feel, it plays an important role in our minds and hearts.

That's where the law of attraction comes into play. Whether we want to lose weight, earn more money, or be happier, the law of attraction says this comes from deep within you. Your thoughts and feelings bring to you what you are, allowing yourself to think about it in any given situation.

Let's look at being frustrated with your outer body, which is just the shell that holds your spiritual being, your soul. Being overweight, from a few pounds to obese, the same thoughts could be following you around inside your head. These defeating thoughts could be manifesting what you don't want, to have extra calories.

Where to Start

It must start within you. That power of your mind is within you. Thoughts are energy, and repetitive thoughts begin to manifest. It's not easy to lose weight, but it is doable. Learn to create and clear your mind of the chatter: "It's too hard, I like to eat, my metabolism is slow, I'm getting older," you know, the thoughts that allow you to be less than you would like to be.

Let your thoughts take you in a different direction. How can you clear these thoughts? When a thought comes into your mind that is negative or that you don't want to hear, say to yourself, "Clear, clear, clear," as soon as you hear it, and replace it with a positive thought or a picture in your mind. You might, for instance, say to yourself, "I am beautiful just the way I am," or you could visualize a beautiful rose in your mind that reminds you of the love you have for yourself.

Set a Goal

When you set a goal for yourself and you write it down or make a vision board with pictures of how you would like your life to look like or feel, it gives permission to the universe to step in and help with the situation. Make your goal clear to yourself and the divine, and make a plan for the goal to come to fruition.

It Takes Work

Everything worth having in our life takes work. It doesn't happen magically or overnight. Goals take time to achieve, one step at a time. No one can make a goal happen for us, but a good support team does help. Find your tribe and surround yourself with those who love you and want to help, not sabotage you. Be happy and have a great attitude as you work on your goal.

Attitude is Everything

Don't waste another day thinking you will be happy when your dreams are realized. Be happy now. Live in this moment, so you don't waste a moment of your life.

Meditation

The power of meditation is miraculous as it brings you into a state of being where everything is positive and your spiritual guides, masters, and all the Divine feels closer. Try meditating for a short time each day, even if it's just a short time. Bumps in the road are going to happen. They make you stronger once you rise above them. It's a blessing to learn how to get over hurdles as they flare up. When you learn the lesson, the lesson can then disappear.

Know that everything doesn't always happen in our timing but rather in God's timing. Don't be hard on yourself. Heaven has a plan. Clear your thoughts, set a goal, keep a positive attitude, do the work, and ask for help. Everyone here and in heaven wants you to be happy and fulfilled, so take that first step and see yourself soar.

Judgmental? Hey, Mediums are Human Too

Dear Bonnie: Do you ever feel that the people who should be the most spiritual can be the most judgmental? I am a working medium as well, and I would think people working with the spiritual world would be nice, but I am surprised at how jealous and mean others can be. What are your thoughts?

I remember when I first started working in this field, how happy I was that I would be working with like-minded people and thought we would all be one big happy family, but I quickly learned that working in the metaphysical world would have its challenges.

When I decided to use my gifts to help others, I sought schools that I could attend, including a very prestigious school in England, but what I found was that putting 50 to 100 psychic mediums together in one room is quite eye-opening. I remember calling one of my friends in New York, who is a working medium, with my concerns, and I listened as she told me the metaphysical world is very competitive and full of jealousy.

I couldn't believe this was the way it was but quickly learned the hard way. We are all human and have these moments of, "I wish that were me," or "How come she gets so much attention?" or "Why isn't my work moving me forward?" But then I remember hearing God's words: "Never mind what everyone else is doing. Put on your blinders and follow your own journey. It's not always so easy."

Judgment doesn't just happen between other mediums. It spills out into many areas of our lives. My husband and I were asked to become members of a local church in my hometown. Our former church had closed, and I thought this was a great opportunity to meet some new people and to help the community I had grown up in. We were asked to attend classes so the pastor could get to know us and vice versa. After the last class, the pastor asked us to go around the table we were sitting at with the other candidates and tell everyone what we did for a living.

I knew saying I was a medium might have its downfall. When my turn came I stated that I was a medium and owned a healing and learning center. The others in the group seemed intrigued. They started to ask questions and seemed to be very interested. I went up to the pastor assuring him that my work as a medium is always with God and the angels, and he seemed fine with that.

One week before the ceremony at which my husband and I were to become members, I was called into the pastor's office. I knew he wanted to talk about my job, but never did I think I was going to hear the words, "You cannot be a member of this church." He blamed the deacons for not wanting me to become a member. I asked him if he had talked to God about his decision, and he replied that he could not hear anything. I was crushed, walking out of a church and being judged for my work helping others.

Living in the same community, I started to run into the deacons of the church, and they were astounded when I told them what happened. A few of them even came to see me for readings, letting me know this was not their doing.

It's so sad to think that people in the metaphysical world, and even the people that we hold to a higher standard, would think of judging each other, but it happens. Be true to yourself and your calling to serve by doing this work. God knows your heart. The rejection crushed me, and then God showed me he doesn't leave you with people who are not going to honor you for you.

Find your own tribe, the people who will hold you up in the highest of regard, and never mind the people who do not. It's all a journey.

Colors Can Affect Your Mood Through Chakras

Dear Bonnie: I know you are a reiki master and work with colors. Do you think changing the colors of your wardrobe can affect your mood? I always wear black but lately have been drawn to lighter, brighter colors.

Colors can very much affect your mood. I, for one, love wearing black, mostly because it's slimming, but when I started on my spiritual journey, I started to learn and feel the difference between the various colors and how they affect us.

Psychologists have studied chromology, the study of how different colors can affect how you think. All colors have different properties and affect your brain differently. The colors of the rainbow are the colors of the seven main chakras in your body. These are your seven main chakras that are the energy centers located from the base of your spine up to the top of your head, your crown chakra.

The base of your spine (your root chakra) is the color red. Red radiates energy and can increase your pulse, at the same time boosting your energy. Wearing red to an interview shows power and strength. This chakra balances your physical energy, motivation, and practicality while promoting a sense of reality. Wear red when you want to feel strong and in balance with the world.

The color orange is the color of the sacral chakra, located in your lower abdomen. It is associated with creativity and used to release stress and blocks in your life.

Yellow, the color of the sun, is a mood-booster and is related to your solar plexus, located in your upper abdomen. Think of wearing yellow when you want to have a day filled with confidence. Yellow reduces anxiety and clears your thoughts. How can you think heavy thoughts when you are wearing a bright-yellow jacket that seems to be beaming with sunshine, which is very healing?

Picture yourself now wearing pink or green, and see yourself wrapped in love and healing. Both colors are associated with your heart chakra, located in the middle of your chest. Green is also associated with feelings of calm and nature. New beginnings and the feeling that life is eternal and growth in all areas of your life stem from the color green.

Pink, meanwhile, is a delicate color associated with love, sweet, romantic, and tenderness. Imagine a bouquet of delicate pink roses being delivered to you and how this would make you feel inside. This is the power of pink, the universal color of love for oneself and others.

Light blue is the color associated with the throat chakra, located in the middle of your throat, and associated with communication. If going on a job interview or giving a speech, wearing a piece of clothing that has the color of light blue opens up your communication abilities, blue being the color that symbolizes loyalty, wisdom, and trust. Blue has a calming effect on the psyche. Imagine, as you close your eyes, looking deep into the blue ocean and then turning your head up and looking at a clear blue sky.

Your brow chakra, in the middle of your forehead, is associated with dark blue. This chakra is about seeing with your mind's eye. It increases intuitive skills and memory. Dark blue is associated with depth and stability. Wear this color when you want to feel a stronger faith and connection to heaven.

The color purple is associated with your crown chakra at the top of your head. Spiritual, physical, and emotional health is what your crown chakra is all about, letting go and letting yourself be guided by the universal life-flow energy that is there for all. Wear the color purple when you want to feel connected to a higher being. Purple is soothing to your soul. It is the color of energy that surrounds your body and has been known to represent creativity, ideas, and enlightenment. The color purple can say a lot about your spiritual, emotional, and physical being.

Each day as you pick out what you are wearing, ask yourself what colors you need to wear to give yourself that extra something to handle whatever you are facing today. Maybe you just want to feel happy as you go about your day, so you choose a little bit of yellow that reminds you of the sun. If you're like me and wear a lot of black, add a scarf or some colorful shoes. I had a celebrity medium tell me if you're going to wear black, wear some colorful underwear.

Whatever you choose, be aware that colors can very much affect how we are feeling. Take the time to see where you can put some color into your day.

Wear the colors of the rainbow and know everything will be as it should be.

Messages from Heaven Clearer Than Sunshine

Dear Bonnie: Have you experienced a sign from heaven that is so clear it cannot be explained away?

There are many signs from our loved ones in heaven that we receive every day, but some come to us in a manner that no one could explain away.

Last week, at a class I was giving in my healing and learning center, a group of students gathered. I began the class with a prayer asking spirit to join us. This class was about communicating with our loved ones and was meant for anyone who wished to learn how to receive a sign on their own. We started with a guided meditation that I created and that I end many group events with. I happen to be making this meditation into a CD, and I call it Love Never Dies.

After the meditation was over and tears were shed, the group formed a circle and we started to work with cards that I made called Messages from Heaven. These 52 cards are messages that I have received from working with spirit, and no two cards are alike.

I taught the class how to shuffle the deck while asking for a message from the loved one they wanted to communicate with while saying their name in their minds. Then I asked them to feel which card was meant for them and to take it out of the deck. Each student sat with a card facing down until everyone was done. We then proceeded to go around the circle, giving the name and relationship of the person on the other side that we wanted to hear from.

Cards are a tool for receiving messages, and they actually work very well. When it was Tom's turn to share, he flipped over his card that read, "You are my sunshine." We all listened to Tom as he told us how his mom had sung that song to him as a boy all the time. Their bond with each other was very strong, and he missed her presence in his life every day.

When I tuned into her energy, she asked me to give him another message: She needed him to know that she still wanted everyone to enjoy

Easter and began showing me a ham with all the fixings. When I spoke the words she was giving me, Tom explained that his mother had passed one year ago on Easter Day, but the sign didn't stop there.

When Tom got home that night he received a picture from his daughter and her mom who were vacationing in Myrtle Beach together and had gotten tattoos that day. Tom sent me the picture he had taken of his card that he had drawn the night before, "You are my sunshine," and the picture he received from his daughter showing their tattoos. The tattoos read on one of the feet, "You are my sunshine" and on the other of his daughter's feet, "My only sunshine."

Tom sent me both pictures together. All I could say was, "Amazing!" Not only did Tom's lovely mom get a message to her son, but she also let him know she was watching his family and keeping them all close together in her heart. She is no longer in the physical world, but very much alive and living life every day with those who she loves.

Make Every Day Meaningful

Dear Bonnie: Sometimes I feel as though I am just going through the steps of life like it's this big race and everything seems to keep going around and around with nothing new happening. It's not what I imagined my life would be, and I never seem to be enough. Do you have any thoughts that could put me on my soul's path?

I do know how you feel. Life can be so exciting at times, and at other times it seems everything is the same day after day, almost like that movie Groundhog Day where the guy keeps waking up to the same day over and over again.

I think these are the times when we need to start dreaming how we would like our life to be and begin to imagine ourselves living the dream we had when we were young, not being afraid or worried about what might happen, a time when we used our imaginations and believed we could be whatever we wanted, the dreams of our younger soul and why we chose to come down to explore this time on Earth.

We can get stuck in a rut if we are not careful, especially when we see our lives not turning out exactly as we imagined they would, each time accepting disappointment instead of seeing it as an opportunity. When we see challenges as opportunities to grow, we can move away from the problem or frustration with new vigor, almost like taking on a new assignment and figuring out how to make lemons into lemonade.

We think we need to follow the rules that society has set for us, the pressure to look like that model on the front cover of the magazine. One gym puts down another and the people in it to gain customers for themselves. Living in a world in which knocking down the dreams of others seems to be okay, it's easy to get caught up in the negativity that surrounds us and makes us look less than perfect.

If you have faith that everything is happening for a greater reason and things may not look like they are supposed to, every decision you make is just a choice that is yours to make because you have God's free will. If you embrace the knowledge that you are perfect just the way you are and dream big for yourself, then you can see the world from a different point of view, just a classroom, not where your soul lives.

Let the soul of that little girl or boy within you explore and learn, dance and feel, be one with yourself and others. Love is the reason you have stepped into this life. You have the choice of waking up each morning feeling like it's Groundhog Day or jumping out of bed with vigor and asking yourself what new adventures will come today.

I'm not saying it's easy, but I am saying it's a decision. So have faith, say a prayer and ask for help from above, then enjoy your day, because one day of our life that isn't meaningful in some way seems wasted when it could have been amazing. This poem came to me a few weeks ago. I think it fits nicely.

Free

Free to be me
To watch the sunrise
In the morning
To see the glow of happiness
On a child's face
To hear the birds
As they swoop down to visit
Free to see the beauty
In all living things
To accept all things
Are possible
And nothing is a given
But everything is
A gift
Free to be me

What Kind of Medium Are You? I Work for God

This week, someone asked me, "What kind of a medium are you? What sets you apart from someone else doing the same thing?"

It took me a moment to think of what this woman was asking, but I can understand the question and how it could be confusing. There does seem to be more and more mediums coming out of every nook and cranny, all offering something a little different.

When I heard the voice of God asking me to make this my profession, He did say He needed more light because the world was becoming darker. With this being the case, why wouldn't God be opening more people all over the world to share this enlightened state to be able to reach as many souls as possible?

The kind of medium I am is the one who feels directly connected to God and the universe. My purpose is to assist and help as many souls as I possibly can so that others may see that there is truly no death. When that fear is taken away, it frees you to be able to believe that life is eternal and love never dies.

Hearing the voice of God has been one of the most precious gifts I have been given, but I truly believe everyone has this ability to open themselves up to this divine knowing and hearing. I call it God and your sixth sense. We were all born with our basic five senses, and your sixth sense is your intuition. We all can tap into this sixth sense of intuition. I always say God didn't send you down to Earth and just say, "Good luck with that."

Your intuition is your seat of all-knowing. Are you tuning in to hear that small voice of knowing? Not everyone hears the big, loud, booming voice of God outside their head. Sometimes it's that small, little whisper inside your head saying, "Maybe that's not a great idea, or maybe not at this time." Sometimes that voice will whisper, "Yes, the timing is right for you to pursue what you have been dreaming about, something that has been on your heart for a long time."

Your crown chakra, located at the top of your head, is the energy center that is the seat of all knowing, the place where all things spiritual come to you. When you take the time to meditate and quiet the mind, you will begin to connect with the Divine. By stopping the chatter of our everyday lives, we open ourselves to be able to tune into the creator of the universe.

God will help you with the small stuff as well as the big stuff. Why? Because He cares for each and every one of us. Ask God to open your spiritual ears to tune into the frequency before you make a decision.

Your solar plexus, located at the top of your abdomen, is the place where you get your gut feelings — God asking you to you pay attention to how you feel when making a decision. Do you feel at peace or unrest with a decision? That's God giving the thumbs-up or -down. Don't ignore these promptings of God. God uses your intuition to guide and protect you while on your journey here. When you become attuned to the voice and messages you receive from above, your journey becomes filled with meaning.

In answering the lady who asked what kind of medium I am, I guess my answer would be, "I work for God." I am not saying I am unique or set apart, but my mission is truly to connect this dimension to the higher side of life, offering a glimpse of heaven to those who need to hear from someone they are missing, helping those who want and need to see, hear, and feel their intuition, so they can tune into that small voice and know that we are never alone on this journey.

Learn to Appreciate What You Have; After All, You Chose This Life

Dear Bonnie: Why does it seem like some have everything and others not enough?

There's a saying that's been out there for a long time; "The only two things you can be sure of are taxes and dying." But in the meantime, there is a lot of life to go through. Your soul came to Earth this time around to experience something or someone that it needed in order to grow, expand, and become more aware.

Have you ever had that feeling of 'I know there must be more'? I think we start to ask ourselves this when we are on our journey. It's going fine, but something deep inside of us knows that something is missing.

Our soul picks who are parents are going to be. Yes, that's right; you picked your mom and dad and the circumstances that you were born into before coming into your earthly situation. Some chose to be born into rich and famous households, while others were born into middle-class families that appear to look like a Normal Rockwell painting.

Then there's the hard-working family that works all the time but never seems to have enough to go around. There are other situations that are far worse than these, and you wonder why any soul would want to come down to Earth and live this existence. It's the hardest situations that offer the most growth. There are learning and growth in each situation that life will bring us through, both the good and the bad.

My mom always told me the grass isn't always greener on the other side. Each of us has his own journey, and sometimes we ponder why our life or situation is the way it is. I have always told my son since he was little that there are always going to be others who have less than you and others who have more.

Your soul has been here many times before. Its mission is to experience different situations, and it has chosen your life the way it is this time on

Earth so it can learn from these different experiences: rich, poor, famous, or an average Joe, hopefully becoming more sympathetic or open-hearted as your soul goes through each situation.

The goal, I believe, is to be at peace with what you have and to be able to understand another's point of view. Can you see someone else's point of view without letting it take the peace inside you? Remember that we are here for just a short time and this is our schoolhouse. We are here to learn, and sometimes it's a challenge.

The next time you are facing a challenge, look at the difficulty from a bird's-eye view and ask yourself, "What is my lesson? What did I want to learn when I chose to come to Earth in my current situation?" By looking at obstacles from a different perspective, you might be able to see the lesson.

When we learn to grow with each new experience, good or bad, our soul is expanding. With each situation you are going through, there is a new opportunity for growth. Take a deep breath, and trust that it will be okay in the end, no matter what the outcome might be.

If you move past and learn from all that is going on around you and face the challenges with a knowing from deep inside that this, too, is a growth spurt, it might take away the fear or worry. Face what you fear and handle the problem from a loving point of view, and notice that the problem or challenge will soon dissipate.

Sometimes we just need to feel that we are enough.

Leaving Your Family Home is Emotional

Dear Bonnie: I am having a hard time saying goodbye to my family home and moving on. Do you think this is crazy? I have all these emotions.

I absolutely know what you are going through. I am so sorry. I know it's hard as I am going through the same thing, and I am sure others have had these same feelings.

This week was a hard week for me, as I had to say goodbye to the family home in which I was brought up. My mother and father purchased a one-room schoolhouse almost 70 years ago. The home is listed in the history books dating back to 1886. My mom, always being proud of this fact, kept the sign explaining its historic significance by the front door.

My mom passed three years ago, and my dad left everything in the house perfectly the same. When he went to heaven a few months ago, my sister and brothers and I needed to go in and clear everything out of the house so we could put it on the market. So much of me wanted to keep that house for myself, but it just wasn't in the cards. Walking in, I knew it would be daunting without seeing my mom or dad waiting for me to come in, as there was always a hug and kiss waiting inside for me.

I moved out of the house when I was fairly young, my mom handing me a key and saying, "A woman should always have a place to go, and this will always be your home."

On the last visit, because the house had sold, I felt the pull to go in say a few words and thank my mom and dad for being such great parents and raising us in an environment where I always felt safe and loved, and in a house that was filled with so many memories.

I was one of five children, and I can still remember us having different bedrooms as the older sibling grew and moved out of the house. I walked through the hall and felt the woodwork for the last time, and not just any woodwork. These boards were the old-fashioned kind, and I could feel the energy of all the years I had laughed, cried, and told stories here, not to mention all the spirits that had kept me company.

I went through each room recalling a particular memory of being in there with each person in my family. I even went into the closet of my first bedroom that I could remember sleeping in and looked into the closet. In there, I found the pink-flowered wallpaper I loved so much, as I remembered laying in my bed as a young girl daydreaming as I looked at the beautiful flowers.

I walked outside and said goodbye to my grandmother's rose bush that still bloomed each year as well as the flower bed my mom loved so much. As I was looking around, my eyes gazed at my dad's apple tree, and I found myself thinking, who will take care of his beloved tree and his blueberry bushes? My dogs and cats were all buried under the trees around the same spot. I know they are no longer there, but who will ever know that they lived and were loved?

Leaving the house for the last time and taking just the memories, I wished and hoped the new owner will feel the love that comes from this house and all the love that went on in the inside.

I read that by walking around the house or home you are leaving and telling the house you are going and that someone new is coming, it releases the energy you have given it and helps the house to welcome the new people that, hopefully, will love it as you have.

If You Feel Spirits, It's Up to You to Hone Your Talents

Dear Bonnie: I began to hear, see, and feel spirits around me only about five or six years ago. I am wondering why my gift began so late in life and what I am supposed to do with it.

Some people remember seeing or hearing spirits at a very early age and then having the ability somewhat disappear until later in life. That sometimes happens if a child who is seeing spirits tells her mom and dad, and it is pushed away instead of embraced. I was lucky, as my mom could also see and receive messages from spirit, so my ability was nurtured.

A lot of parents come to me describing their children talking to someone as if they are having a conversation, but they are not sure who it is until their child points to a picture of grandpa hanging on the wall and the child says, "That's grandpa. He visits and has tea with me when I am playing." Instead of saying, "That's just your imaginary friend," they sense that grandpa is visiting his grandchild and the gift is welcomed.

What might have happened is your case is that you're a sensitive person but didn't realize your gift was there until something triggered you to become open, like the passing of a loved one, which can open you up to the spiritual world. Some others have a near-death experience that makes them more sensitive to the other side.

Without talking to you, I cannot be sure why you are sensing spirits at this time. It is totally up to you to embrace this sixth sense that is happening to you, or you can ask for it to be taken away. We all have God's free will, and if you ask, I believe you will receive. If, however, you feel you can help others and yourself by using these gifts, then I would suggest getting some training so you know how to use your gift and understand what is happening.

Seeing, hearing, or sensing spirit can be overwhelming if you're not sure what to do. Training is a must if you want to learn how to control what is happening and where. I have heard others say that they have no control over when they receive messages, but there is a way to control what you're

91

receiving and by whom. If you are unable to attend workshops or schools, there are some great teachers on the internet and YouTube. Be sure to do your research on who you can trust and learn from.

Another great way to start is to visit a bookstore, pick out a book that you are attracted to, and start reading about mediumship and psychic abilities, becoming familiar with the dialogue. If you decide to go further, you can seek a metaphysical teacher and start to train on honing your gifts.

Most mediums feel they are called to do this work to be in service to others. Whatever you decide, make sure it feels right for you.

If I'm Seeing Spirits, What Am I Supposed to Do With this Gift?

Dear Bonnie: I've started to see, hear, and feel spirits around me, but only for the last few years. I wonder what I am supposed to do with this gift. Was I given the gift to help others? How do I get started with building my abilities? My children are young and seem to see and hear them as well. Any information would be helpful.

Let's start with your gift. I knew I had the gift since the early age of four, as I can remember seeing, hearing, and feeling spirit around me. This is the same for a lot of other mediums as well. It seems to be the age of knowing that the spirit world does exist. Children up until the age of seven usually can see the spirit world as they are newly here from heaven.

Lots of loved ones come through while I am giving a reading and ask me to acknowledge the little ones that have come into the world after their passing. They often reveal to me that they are spending time with the children, talking and playing with them. The children can very much have a relationship with them from the other side. So if you see your child sitting at their princess table serving tea and talking to what seems to be their imaginary playmate, it just might be a grandpa in heaven.

If your gift seems to be revealing itself later, you might not be remembering the times you have had at a young age, or your gift has opened just when you're ready to take the next step of strengthening your abilities. I also have heard from other mediums that their third eye center, which is the center located in the middle of your forehead and is the center for clear-seeing, has been opened either by a near-death experience or the passing of a loved one. I believe they both can be a catalyst for helping someone become even more sensitive to the spiritual world.

The spiritual world is all around us, and we all can tune into this world. Sometimes it's a matter of whether we want to and whether we are ready. We are all made up of energy, and energy never goes away; we just move into another dimension.

There are several ways to develop your abilities. Some like to study either online or by reading spiritual books. Some like to choose a teacher or mentor to work with. When I started years back, I had been reading books by a popular medium and then went to a class where he was teaching. A group environment is helpful because while you are learning there are always other students to practice exercises. Whichever way feels best to you is the right way. Follow your gut instinct.

I love giving classes at my center and seeing new people join our group and begin to grow their psychic gifts. It's amazing to watch as their eyes light up as they deliver their first message from the divine and realize that we are not on this journey alone.

I believe this gift is given to help others in the world and also to fill us with the knowledge that while we are here on Earth, guidance can be given with love and caring from the Divine.

Loss of Parents is Painful, But They are Still With You

Dear Bonnie: I have lost people in my life who mean a lot to me, and I know it is painful, but my dad passed this year, and I seem to be having a harder time getting through it. I know it takes time, but I wake up feeling sad about him every morning. I seem to be better during the day at work, but then a thought squeaks in, and I am sad all over. Are there some ways of coping that you can suggest?

Loss is a given during our lifetime. Some losses we seem to be able to deal with, and they seem to be more manageable, but others seem to take a hold on our lives and every aspect of it, and the grieving process takes hold of us. Recognizing that you have a loss is the first step and then finding ways to deal with that loss at this moment.

Most of us have felt losses throughout our lives, starting when we are children. A beloved pet, a grandparent that we love, or even the loss of moving to a new town and leaving behind friends can be significant losses. As we age, we see loss through divorce, jobs that end, friendships that we had as children disappearing because of time and growing apart. We mourn for the way things used to be.

The one constant in our lives seems to be our parents and the idea that they are never going to disappear from our lives. My mom's passing three years ago was a massive loss for me, and I seemed to turn all my energy and focus on helping my dad, who was 90 at the time. It seemed to cushion the despair of losing my mom with caring for my dad. This year I lost my dad, and with no one to take up that time and energy, I felt the loss so much more. The thought that I no longer have parents here on Earth seemed daunting, even to me, a medium who can see spirit on the other side.

Acknowledging your loss first to yourself and then sharing your feelings with others is a big step. There always seems to be someone who knows how you are feeling and having someone you can openly share your grief with is essential. Holding it inside and letting it fester is not good for your soul or your body.

I do know that life goes on for your dad, just in a different way, and that the bond between the two of you can never be broken. My advice to my clients is to bring their loved ones on their life journey. Your loved ones in spirit love it when you are smiling and dancing as they dance by your side. They walk in the sand by the ocean with you and join you as you stand to look out the window, watching the cardinal they have sent your way, one of just a few signs that they are with you still.

I am not a grief counselor, but here are a few tips that might make things a little easier for you.

1. Take the time you need to be sad. They're your feelings; acknowledge them.
2. Talk to others about your feelings.
3. Find a ritual that will help you to honor them.
4. Visit the grave if it helps. They hear you no matter what, but if it helps to have a peaceful place to talk to them, they feel honored.
5. Plant flowers or a tree in their memory.
6. Light a white candle, and say a prayer, as prayers are heard. They say prayers for you as well.
7. Create an altar or a place in your home where you can place a picture, play their favorite music, place some flowers, and ask their spirits to join you, then acknowledge their presence. Speak to them like they are there because they are.
8. If a tattoo is your way of keeping them close, they know about them also. It is doing something that makes you feel better.

I remember when my mom passed, I took a pair of her slippers home with me and wore them to bed for a full year. When my husband and I went to see Theresa Caputo, the Long Island Medium, at a big event she was giving, I was amazed to hear her last words before she left the stage: "There is a mom here who wants to acknowledge that her daughter has been wearing her slippers to bed at night for the last year." I loved receiving that message, and it was a piece of evidence that only my mom and I could have known about, confirming for me that she knew my ritual.

I also found relief in going to a spiritualist church that I belong to and receiving messages from my parents from other mediums. Whatever faith you believe in, I feel that the bond with God and the universe helps to lessen the pain in the knowledge that our loved ones are safe and sound. Do what makes you feel better, knowing they are with you still, guiding and watching with love, the kind of love that never leaves us and is everlasting.

At an event I was hosting this past weekend, a husband from the spirit world bent down close to his wife in the audience and handed her a card showing me he was drawing hearts on it. As I explained what I was seeing, the wife said, "Every year my husband made me a handmade Valentine's card that he would draw hearts on and give to me." Who would know that? It was so touching to watch the love that was still so strong between this couple.

Loved Ones Send Signs; It's Up to Us to Read Them

Dear Bonnie: I hear about certain signs that our loved ones can send after they pass. Can you mention a few more and what they might mean? I feel my dad is trying to get a message to me, but I am not quite sure what it means.

Messages can be quite subtle. Sometimes you know they are from a specific person, and you feel the message in your heart. I believe that when someone passes, the first thing they want to do is send us a sign to let us know they have arrived at their destination, heaven.

It's like when you were a teenager, and your mom and dad started to let you go out with your friends, but they wanted to make sure you were safe and sound, so you needed to call and check in occasionally. Our loved ones do not want us to have a worry or be left with the thought that they have died and it's the end of them being in our lives. It's very much the opposite; they now have the ability to see, hear, and know what is going on with us.

Souls that pass have the choice of going into the white light where their loved ones are waiting, or, if they choose, they can take their time to check in on family members and friends before they transition to their heavenly home. We have God's free will; it is their choice. Sooner more than often later, they will see that white light and someone patiently waiting for them and the transition will happen.

Before my dad passed, I was in my dream time and in the energy space where spirit can show you many things. I came to realize I was being shown a room where all of my dad's family were waiting for him. His mother had passed when he was just four, and I had only seen pictures of her. I have one particular picture of her and my grandfather together sitting on my hutch in my dining room, and when I recognized her, she stood up from where she was sitting with the rest of the family and began to wave frantically to me as she knew I could see her.

She looked exactly like she did in my picture, showing me her beautiful smile as she was so happy to acknowledge that we were seeing each other and having a connection. It was a happy moment, but I began to realize that what I was seeing was my dad's family preparing for him and waiting to greet him when he arrived. I was both happy and sad.

Two days later, after my dad went to be in heaven, I was sitting in the living room. I became aware of the smell of smoke around me. I jumped up out of my chair to see if anything was burning. One of the psychic gifts is called clairolfactory, or clear smell. It's just one way of receiving a message. Someone might be able to smell a grandmother's perfume or a father's aftershave. It's associated with a spirit person.

So, after checking my house to see if there was a fire and realizing there was nothing burning, I sat back in my chair, and the smell of smoke came back again, stronger this time. It took me a moment to realize that it was my dad's message to me: The smoke represented the wood stove my dad kept constantly going in his home. He loved his wood-burning stove in his kitchen. He loved the warmth and feel of contentment that it brought into his life.

As soon as I caught on, I smiled to myself and said out loud. "Dad, I know it's you, thank you for the sign. I know you're safe and sound." I was still sad but happy to know he was with his mom and family who he had longed to see.

There are many signs, and usually they mean something to both you and your loved one who has passed. They are a way of sharing a memory, bringing comfort to those who are left behind in the physical world.

Other signs may come from your ability to clear-taste. This ability is called clairgustance, the ability to psychically taste a substance, liquid, or food without actually putting anything in your mouth. You might be able to taste your loved one's favorite food or a cigarette or pipe they smoked.

Stay aware of the things going on around you after the passing of a loved one or when you feel sad. Everyone in heaven knows our thoughts and will try to communicate one way or another.

Like I always say, love never dies, and your loved ones are always connected to you, just in a different way but always from the heart. When you receive a sign, acknowledge it and give thanks to the spirit you feel is sending the sign. It is just a new way to keep the conversation and relationship alive until we meet again.

Best Reading is When Medium, Client, and Spirit Work Together

Dear Bonnie: I would like to go for a reading. I am wondering what makes one reading better than another, and what I should expect during a reading. Do you think life goes on as usual in heaven?

As a medium trained by some of the most renowned mediums in the U.S. and the U.K., I was always taught the same method: give what you get, meaning spit out what comes through. Because even though it doesn't mean anything to you, it might mean something to your sitter (the person coming in for the reading).

We try to be as forthright with the information as we can, knowing the message is not for us, not trying to make sense of the information, but giving the information as it comes through from our communicator.

At the beginning of the reading, besides saying a prayer, I will tell my client a few pieces of information that might make their reading a little easier. First, I tell everyone to sit with an open mind and heart. Everything is energy, and when the sitter is open to receiving, the energy flows easier. Nerves or someone heavily grieving may block the communication or make the reading a little more difficult.

I also let them know their loved one in heaven can come through looking younger than when they passed. We go back to a time when we felt and looked our best. I tell my clients that when a medium someday sees me, I am going to be in a bikini because I haven't been able to wear one for a long time. That makes them laugh and opens communication.

I might see a dad who passed in his 90s coming through looking 18 and in his sailor's uniform. They usually appear to me knowing this is how you would best recognize them, sometimes showing me a picture of themselves that you have recently been looking at.

A reading is personal to everyone, and I tell my clients that their loved one is not coming to talk to me, but to them. The best reading, I believe, is one where the communicator in spirit is familiar with how the process works with me on this side, meaning they blend well with my energy, and I can see, hear, and feel their presence. As they come close beside me, blending their energy with mine, we become one.

I strive for this every time I give a reading, but it's not always that easy. Because they have the same personality as they had while on Earth, some communicators are full of fun and some are much more conservative. You know the feeling; some people are just easier to talk to.

My job is to let your loved one know I am here for them as the middleman, just delivering the message. I have had communicators start to give me advice as well, which I love; it means they are trusting me. The best reading is when you feel in your soul that you have talked to someone's loved one in heaven, it was he or she speaking, and you have just had a conversation with that someone.

I will always remember a post on Facebook that read, "Just came from a reading with Bonnie Page and it felt like I had an hour-long visit with my dad." I was so happy I could give someone this gift.

What comes through for information is very much the communicator's job of what he or she wants us to say. Some clients come in with one particular event or subject they want their loved one to say, and that can be sad because if they cannot relay that exact information or it is something they do not want to bring up, it can ruin your beautiful message. Sometimes they do understand what is important to you, and they do a smashing job at relaying the info.

I was talking to a client to whom I had given a telephone reading quite a few months prior, and he told me about what he had asked his mom to mention during the reading. He told me the reading was spot on the whole time, and he was grateful that he knew it was his mom, but she had not revealed the one piece of information he had asked her earlier during the day.

He told me as I was closing the phone reading, I said, "Wait. Your mom wants to tell you she is playing cards in heaven." There was silence on the other end. He couldn't speak, because that was the piece of information he was waiting for as he had been holding the deck of cards in his hand the whole time. Good job, mom. If I would have left that little bit of information out, it would have been a good reading but maybe not an amazing reading.

Playing cards in heaven with the family and friends they played with here on Earth shows that life goes on in heaven as on Earth. It's comforting to know we very much continue to live on the other side. Our souls are eternal and everlasting. They miss us but have a bird's-eye view as they watch over us, enjoying our lives with us.

Signs are Everywhere, Even in a Fortune Cookie My Message from Dad

Dear Bonnie: I try to stay focused on a spiritual path, but sometimes I seem to slip off and find my ego calling the shots. It's hard to be spiritual when something happens for a colleague that you have been trying to succeed at, and it's not happening for you. I find myself jealous, and resentment slips in, and I know that is not being very spiritual. What should I do?

Last week in my center, I was giving a reading to a woman who was getting a message from her dad in heaven. He kept giving me pictures of horses and then showing me a saddle and some ribbons: red, to be exact. It turns out he was an avid rider and had been in many horse shows and won many ribbons.

After the reading was complete, we continued to talk about how her dad had raised horses to show at events. My dad also had raised and raced racehorses. We continued talking about standard breeds and thoroughbreds and the difference between the two, how our dads had so much in common, and the bond between our dads and ourselves.

That night, my son called me as I was leaving work and asked if my husband and myself would join him at a Chinese restaurant we love. We had an amazing meal, and at the end, the server brought our fortune cookies. I opened mine and started to laugh as I read the words: "Anyone can 'start,' only the thoroughbred will 'finish'!"

I took that little fortune, slipped it into my pocket, and brought it home, knowing it not only had a more significant meaning but also that my dad had been at and heard the reading I had given that same day. If I weren't amazed enough, I felt something inside of me saying that this is going to mean more to you. I took that little piece of paper home and pinned it up on a mirror, telling my dad in my mind, "Okay. I am listening and I received your sign."

It didn't end there, though. Two days later I would need these words of encouragement as I got the news that some goals I have been trying to achieve would take a little longer than I had expected. Walking around my home, feeling disappointed for myself, I heard a little voice inside my head say, "Go look at your fortune. Anyone can 'start,' only the thoroughbred will 'finish!'"

Oh my, not only did these words have the encouragement I needed to hear, but also left me with the message, "We are here in spirit supporting you. Things might not be happening as fast as you would like, but keep going ahead and someday you will be at the finish line. A steady pace is what will get you to the finish line. Spirit knows all, not only about the future but also how to get you there."

If you look for the signs, they are there, even in a cookie. Words and signs from heaven are all around you. Don't give up. Be the one who finishes what you started. God always tells me, "Put on your blinders; straight ahead and don't let your earthly feelings get the best of you."

You are loved, and no one wants you to achieve your goals more than everyone in heaven. Listen as they cheer you on.

Spirit Guides are There to Help — Try to Get in Touch

Dear Bonnie: Can you give me some advice on connecting with my guides? I am not sure who is guiding me and what role they can play in my life at this time. I feel someone from spirit is there, but I'm lost when it comes to finding out who they are and what messages they are trying to convey to me.

All of us have guides that have a hand in directing us from the higher side of life. Some guides are with us from birth to when we return home at the end of our life; then some guides come in and out at different times depending on what lessons we have chosen for ourselves, or even when learning new hobbies, jobs, or talents.

Not all guides do everything. Some specialty guides step in and help us with things that they were masters at when they were here on Earth. Guides take on the job of helping others achieve their goals and desires. How do they do that, you wonder? If you have an idea of writing a book or becoming a public speaker, a guide would be assigned to you that has already mastered what you hope to achieve, offering wisdom and knowledge by directing you in the path that would lead you to success.

They send ideas and thoughts to you while you are sleeping, doing a meditation, or by giving you feelings of what your next step might be. Your guides do not tell you what to do but can suggest the best outcome for you. If you have a fear of taking the next step in your career, they might work with you on your self-esteem by placing you in situations that would build up your confidence and surround you with people who would nurture your desires to help you grow.

Guides have been with you your entire life and will never leave your side. Our loved ones in heaven can become our strongest guides as they love us and are invested in our journey. It's almost like watching your child grow up before your eyes here on the Earth plane. When our loved ones pass to the higher side of life, they very much have an interest in making your time here all that it can be for the growth of your soul. Your journey means everything to them.

My guide once told me I can shine a light but not change the situation. We have control; they are there to lend a helping hand.

If you want to build a connection with your guides, the best way to start is meditation. When we take the chatter out of our minds, it makes room for the signs and conversation our guides want to share with us. Take time every day, even if it is for 20 minutes, to clear your mind so the conversation can manifest.

When you are in a meditative state, that is the time to ask who is guiding you. One of many guides may give you their names, appear to you, or send a sign or symbol. If it doesn't happen at first, give it time and have patience. Don't give up; everyone has guides, and it might take a while to get to know them on a personal level and to experience exactly how they are guiding you, but they will try hard to make their presence known.

Life gets easier with the knowledge that you are never alone on your journey.

Native American Spirit Guide Helps Her Through a Lot; Meeting my Spirit Guide as a Child

Dear Bonnie: Do you believe everyone has a guide? I have been seeing a Native American in my dreams, and I am wondering how I can know if he is a guide and how I can build a relationship with him.

I too have a Native American as a guide. The first time I saw him was as a young child. We lived out in a rural area in a small town, and I took the school bus back and forth to school. One day, getting off the bus and running toward the front door of my home, I gazed over at our front porch to see a big Native American sitting on the front porch. I know my mouth dropped open as I could see his frame and face so clearly.

My mom, who also has the gift of clairvoyance (or clear seeing), was looking at me at the same time. She could see him sitting there as well. The term for what my mother was doing is called linking in. She could see what was happening and called out to me, saying, "It's all right. He waits for you to get off the bus every day."

Through the years, I would see this same man in my dream time; he would appear and show me his face, at times coming so close I could see the deep wrinkles that lined his face. I knew he was a man of great importance and well-respected. Even though he seemed strong and silent, I knew he had a kind and loving heart.

One day while meditating, I slipped into a serene sense of peace, and as I came back to consciousness, I could see him once again, but this time he seemed to be sitting. As he disappeared from my vision, I heard the word "Sitting."

Confused as to why he would leave me with those words, I continued with my day when the second word came: "Bull." I realized he was telling me his name was Sitting Bull. Becoming excited as I realized who my guide was, I wanted to know more.

I called my father and asked him if he knew the story of Sitting Bull and then Googled his name, wanting to know more about my lifetime guide. He has appeared through the years, showing me his face in my dream time or meditations to let me know he has stayed with me.

I am not sure exactly why our guides choose us, but I do know from listening to the spirit world that it is a process that is not taken lightly. I recently watched a movie that just came out about the life of Sitting Bull, and at the end of the film, seeing his death, my heart became heavy with grief.

That night, when I was in my dream time, I began to see tall trees and a forest. Soon, my guide appeared on his favorite white horse. He was riding through the woods but stopped his horse in front of me, letting me see his proud and strong face. He sent me his thoughts; he was with Great Spirit in the spiritual world. I knew he was reassuring me.

I do know each of us has a guide — sometimes more than one — who watch over our journey here on Earth. If you want to have a relationship with your guide, meditation is the number-one way of connecting. There are many guided meditations for meeting your guides.

Remember to ask your guide his or her name before you start the meditation, so your connection will become strong and you can feel comfortable calling to him or her when you need strength and protection.

When You Need an Angel, You Ya Gonna Call?

Dear Bonnie: I would like to get to know and feel the angels around me. Do you have a suggestion of where I should start? I do believe in them. I heard there are angels for different jobs.

When I started to get serious with my training in the metaphysical world and how to connect on a higher level, I started out reading everything I could about angels. I purchased as many books on angels that seemed to speak to me, and I started my journey into finding out about these beautiful beings who were created by God as his messengers. We hear about angels stepping in to save someone from danger. We see pictures of angels in churches and places that we visit. But there is so much more to learn.

As a child, I found myself attracted to anything that had pictures of angels, and as I grew up and moved into my first apartment, I found myself buying statues of angels and placing one in each room where they could be seen. I seemed to find comfort with the knowledge that they seemed to be watching over me.

I would learn later that when we surround ourselves with pictures or statues of angels, they feel invited, almost like a calling card of sorts, to let them know we are open to being in their presence. So as I started to learn more about each angel, I picked up a deck of angel cards as well. I would read about the angels every night before bed, even bringing the book or cards with me and setting them on my nightstand.

This seemed to open a doorway for the angels, and one by one they started to communicate with me. I found it surprising that I could see, hear, and talk to the angels. The first angel that came to me was Metatron, and he told me his brother Sepheron was with him. The messages were clear; God wanted me for something special. I said OK, and he was off.

Then, night after night, I would see angels. I know this sounds unbelievable; it even amazed me. The first night that Archangel Michael awoke me, I could see him very clearly, and on the other side of me was a more prominent, framed angel, Archangel Raphael. They each had their own unique look and tone of voice, each with a separate purpose of appearing to me.

Archangel Michael is the protector, with his sword of light and love. He uses this sword to swipe away energy that might have attached to you that should not be there. I hear Michael's voice very well, and he is the angel that I can hear as I pull angel cards for readings. When I first realized I could listen to him as well, as if I were having a conversation with my best friends who were sitting in the same room with me, I kept talking to him for two days, afraid that if I dropped the connection, I wouldn't be able to hear him the same again.

Frequently, I am asked what an angel looks like. Very much like you or I, except sometimes I do see their wings.

Archangel Raphael is very much involved with me, as he is a healer. When I am giving a reiki session, he has been known to show up beside the reiki bed and assist in healings. I have seen him place his two beautiful wings on top of someone as the person lay receiving healing. I am amazed at this as much as you might be as you're reading this. He works very closely with those who are helping to heal others. I also call him or Jesus, who is also a master healer, when I am not feeling well.

Ask your angels for what you need help with; they are never far away.

How to Stay Positive in a Time of Crisis

Dear Bonnie: With all the recent news about what is going on in our world today, do you have any spiritual ways to keep our thoughts and feelings grounded and not all over the place? I know you say not to be fear-based, and I am trying to stay positive.

Every day can be a scary day if that's what we let our thoughts lead us to. It is the right thing to be cautious in times of crisis, but there are some things we can do to stay positive even in times of tragedy or when we are fearful. Begin each day by giving the world, your family, and yourself a blessing. Prayers are heard, and thoughts are energy. By starting with a positive affirmation or saying a prayer or blessing, you are beginning your day with hope in your heart.

Maybe you are blessed with a family you can count on or a beautiful grandbaby or a best friend who you can tell all your deepest secrets and know that they are safe. Start with remembering all the blessings that have been bestowed to you. Focus on the positive as it will automatically push the negative thoughts away.

Come up with a word or phrase that can help you stay focused when a negative or scary thought comes into your head. These words can be short like joy, peace, love, patience, humanity, gratitude, or a longer phrase, like, "Please bless us all with a miracle."

Positive words are empowering, and they can help you stay soul-centered. Those positive words are felt deep inside your soul, and as you think of the task at hand for the day, your soul will remain in alignment with the vibrations of positivity.

Negative thoughts will bring your vibration down, whereas positive thoughts raise your vibration. Practice raising your vibration during the day by taking one task at a time and adding a positive spin to it. There are many ways to increase your vibration, and when doing so, you are aligning your chakras, which are your main energy centers in the body. When you keep your chakras running as they are supposed to run and in alignment, your body has a healthier, happier approach to living.

Raise your vibration by eating healthy, colorful fruits, and vegetables. While making the bed or working out, play some music that gets your energy going and makes you feel like dancing. Dancing and exercising greatly improve your state of being by moving your body and putting a smile on your face. Watch a funny movie, your favorite comedian, or a funny show on TV.

Raising your vibration is about doing the things that bring you enjoyment and that are fun. We each must do our part when it comes to our happiness. Have faith and trust that we do not always know what is going on in the big picture of life.

Accompanying the column is a sketch of an angel and a little saying I wrote for Facebook this weekend. I hope you enjoy her. Please give her a name.

"I give you an Angel to keep by your side.
She is here for all times,
Good times or bad times she won't leave your side.
Make her your own personal guide.
As she protects you and guides you from Heaven above,
God sends his angels, so you know you are loved.
Protecting, guiding, and shining their light
Angels watch over you all day and all night."

Celebrity Spirits Sometimes Send Signals

Dear Bonnie: Have you ever had a celebrity visit, or has a celebrity ever come through while you were giving a message to a client?

I have never attempted to talk to a celebrity just because I wanted to see if I could. However, I have had celebrity visits. I will share with you some of them. I seem to have celebrities who were a little before my time but that I do know about or have seen in old movies, some coming to share details with me. I did not ask; they just appeared to have answers to questions I have had in my real life.

One night, I went to sleep thinking about how I wanted my hair to be styled and colored. I was going to ask my hairstylist, as I had an appointment the next morning, and during the night I awoke to see Marilyn Monroe before me. She did not say anything, but I knew she was showing me her hair. It was short, stylish, and very blond, and I knew she was trying to get that color to me in hopes it would help me with my hair decisions.

The next morning, I went to my stylist and, lo and behold, she had a picture of Marilyn Monroe next to her station. I took her advice, and I still have that same blond hair to this day. You might ask yourself why Marilyn Monroe would care about my hair. I do not know that for certain, but I do know a soul is a soul. She had a sweet presence about her, and I think she thought her color would look good on me.

Visits do not have to be life-changing but always seem to be helpful. Now, would I call up and ask Marilyn Monroe to have a chat with me? No, I would not. But I sure liked seeing her and receiving her advice on my beauty choices.

Another celebrity visit came from Bing Crosby. It was around Christmas time, and I have his Christmas CDs and were listening to them one afternoon. That evening, as I went to bed, I had the question in my mind about a legal matter that was taking place, and when I would be getting notice of the outcome.

That night Bing appeared to me. He nodded his head as if to say,

"Hello," put on his fedora and said, "March 15th." That was it. He left me with a date that, in the morning, I remembered very clearly. A letter came on that exact day, letting me know what the outcome was on that matter. Wow!

What does that prove? The spirit world knows what is going to happen before we do, and Bing was on the money with that one. Even I was amazed at the accuracy of that date, because I live in a small town, and we never know when our mail is coming, as sometimes it takes longer than average.

Another time, while driving to work, very much awake this time, Robin Williams spoke to me like he was sitting next to me riding shotgun. It was just after his tragic passing, and I could hear his voice so clearly. I loved watching all his TV shows and movies and had just watched a video he had made a week before.

His tragic passing had taken me by surprise as he always looked so happy. Robin, however, had a request to deliver a message to someone, and we chatted for a few minutes, and I told him I probably would not be able to reach this person for a few reasons. Imagine someone calling you out of the blue and telling you they have a message for you?

He understood and, even though I felt terrible that I could not help, he reassured me it was OK. And then he was gone, and once again I was alone in my car, driving to work. These stories go to show that we are all one and always connected on some level, on Earth as in heaven, although in heaven, we get to see the bigger picture of why some things work out and others do not. Our egos do not hold us, and we are of pure light.

What I have learned from these experiences and why I am sharing them with you is because it is not the job that you hold here on Earth that makes you who you are, but the love in your heart that makes you a good person, the person who might give a stranger some help with her hair or the exact date of an occasion that will take place, taking away worry from someone you have never met.

It might even be asking for help from someone who doesn't know, but being able to see the compassion in someone's heart that they might be able to help you.

Psychic Circle Will Bring Spirit 'Round

Dear Bonnie: Can you tell me what a psychic message circle is and who should learn to build their abilities? As a small child, I psychically saw spirit with my eyes, but would become frightened and ended up pushing the visions away. Can I bring back these visions now that I am older?

I have clients who come in almost daily telling me the same thing, telling me about the times they have experienced visions or voices, or had a premonition but didn't know what to do with these experiences and became frightened, hence pushing their sixth sense away.

Since the age of four I have seen spirit, sometimes walking around in my family home or at night in my dream time. I couldn't sleep unless I had a light on in my room until the age of 14 because I could sense spirit all around me. I would leave my bedroom door open, hoping to hear my dad snoring two doors down in his room; this always seemed to comfort me.

The only difference that I had as a child was that my mom could see, hear and feel also, and when spirit was visiting, my mom could see what I was seeing, and she would say, "Oh, that's just so-and-so." Maybe they were one of my guides or a relative who had passed. She said it so nonchalantly that I thought everyone was seeing spirit walking around.

The daytime was a piece of cake, but nighttime still a little scary. I never liked dolls as a child, so I didn't have many, but there were times I would get them as presents. At night, I would put them in my mom and dad's room because I would swear they could get up, open their eyes, and start walking around. I guess I figured my mom and dad were the spirit police. This still makes me laugh because the scene I am describing became a movie when I was in high school; someone else was thinking or seeing this also.

Spirit absolutely can use anything they need to get through with a message, but my mom always told me, "It's not the dead you need to be afraid of, it's the living!" As I grew older and started school, I learned that you didn't talk about seeing spirit with your classmates. Spirit communication comes easier to us until the age of seven when our antilocal brain takes over as we start school.

Mine didn't go away, because at home I could talk freely about what I was being shown. It was a blessing to be born into a spiritual family that talked about spirit openly. Everyone is born with psychic ability, but if it is not used, it can become dormant. It's like a muscle; you can build them up, but if you no longer use them, they can become weak.

Psychic message circles are for anyone wishing to build their connection to spirit in a safe atmosphere where everyone wants to do the same. When you learn how to open up your psychic centers and use your intuition, it makes life's decisions a little easier. Some students come to circle knowing they want to use their intuition for guidance, and others wish to make the connection to the spirit world.

I cannot speak for other teachers, only myself, but my classes are always given to help us feel that connection so that we know we are never alone and are very much being guided on our journey. It's incredible to be able to tap into that feeling of knowing we are never left alone on our path, but that help is always there if we ask.

Some students do have advanced abilities and still want to build on what they see, hear, and feel to help themselves and others. It's very healing for both parties to be able to share advice or a message from the spirit world and the divine. Everyone has these psychic centers, and a great way to build your psychic ability is to attend a class or circle. It's never too late to start.

What Does Heaven Look Like?

Dear Bonnie: What do you think heaven looks like, and do our loved ones watch over us?

I was giving a reading last week to a woman who came in asking to speak with her father. The reading started the way it usually does, with me giving evidence that her dad had come to speak with her. I always give a description of the person in heaven that is before me. As I tune into the person's energy field in heaven, I feel if they are joyful or maybe a little stoic. Whatever one's personality was here, it is still very much intact on the other side.

When my client's dad started to show me a boat on a lake surrounded by water, trees, and a small cabin, I described in detail what I was seeing. The daughter said they used to rent a cabin on a lake every summer while dad was alive. As I continued to talk to her dad he said, "This is my version of heaven. I need her to know this is my reality and what I surround myself with every day."

You see, her dad loved being at the lake on vacation with his family, but, unfortunately, one week a year was all the time he had on Earth to enjoy himself with his family the way he wanted to. Now in heaven, he surrounded himself with memories of those times and how much he cherished them.

He did have a regret of not spending more time with his family and saw that his idea of being a good husband and father was providing for them so that they would never be without the things he thought they needed. On the higher side of life, he was things with a different perspective and wanted his daughter to know he wished he had spent more time with her and his family.

As his daughter began to weep gently, he assured her he was there now, watching her family grow and not missing out on any family events. He provided me with proof of birthdays and weddings, even showing me how he had been talking to her daughter, his granddaughter, keeping her company by playing tea with her as she sits at her little pink table and chairs. "Oh! That's who she has been talking to!" the woman said.

I informed her that her dad was very much still in their lives and relaying the message to make sure everyone in the family makes the effort to go to the get-togethers, as they are the most important times in our lives. "Make memories," he told his daughter, "The rest will follow."

Cherished times and memories cannot be taken away and will continue as you create your version of heaven. Enjoy your life now and create a beautiful heaven while you're at it. Love is the most important thing in life.

A Medium's World; My Answers to Your Questions

Dear Bonnie: Could you answer some questions for me? I do not know a lot about what you do, but I believe I have some of the abilities that you have.

Here are some of your questions asked and my answers to them. I hope they help you to understand.

What is a medium? A medium is a person who can communicate with the spiritual world — loved ones, guides, master teachers, such as Jesus and, for me, God — the ability to see, hear, and feel the spiritual world and have a conversation. A medium acts as a middleman for those who wish to seek guidance and need some help with communication.

What was it like sleeping at night when you were a child? Was it scary? From the time I was four years old, I have memories of talking to the spirit world. That did make for some scary nights, as I felt spirits all around me. I was not scared when I saw someone from the spirit world — that always felt comforting — but the feeling that was there when I was sensing them did make me a little fearful. I slept with a full light on until I was 14.

What did your family think of your ability as a child? Were you shunned in any way? I was brought up in a very spiritual home, as I am a fourth-generation medium on my mother's side, so all of it just seemed normal. My mom always encouraged me and my gifts, and my dad, who did not see them, always wondered why we could see and talk to the spirit world, and he could not. He would always say, "How come I cannot see them?" I always would reply, "Because you are not mom's kid."

What are dead people like? They are not really dead and are very much living a fully productive and happy life, just not on this dimension that we are on. Their personalities still shine through, even showing me their sense of humor and unique qualities that make them who they are. My mission is to prove that heaven and our loved ones are alive.

When did you realize you wanted to use your gift to help others? That did not come until later in life. I owned a salon called Bonnie's Class Act, where I did facials for my clients. One day as I was giving a facial, the client's loved one from heaven appeared, and I stopped the facial and was staring into her mother's face. My client said, "Bonnie, what is wrong?" I replied, "There is a lady here."

My client, knowing I was spiritual said, "What does she want?" I telepathically asked the lady some questions, like why she was here and what she wanted her daughter to know. I repeated this to my client, and she became so overwhelmed with joy, she forgot about her facial. After that, spiritual happenings started to happen more often. I began to receive calls about giving readings, and they became more important than my facials.

And that is how my current business, Messages from Heaven, was born.

About the Author

Bonnie Page has become an international medium delivering messages to those around the Globe. Bonnie has a gentle, loving, and sometimes humorous approach while connecting her clients to the spirit world with compassion and integrity.

A born medium with conscious memories of spirit communication since the age of four, Bonnie has developed her talents to become a sought-after evidential medium bringing much joy and peace to many.

In 2014, Bonnie heard the voice of God, who asked her to make her gift her full-time profession when she asked why she heard because the world is becoming a darker and darker place, and we need more light.

She opened "Messages from Heaven Healing and Learning Center," where she delivers private and group messages to those in need. She also offers Zoom and FaceTime readings.

Bonnie truly has a gift for teaching! She is a Reiki Master/Teacher New Age Speaker/ Mentor and Coach. Offering classes aimed at helping others to build their intuitive and metaphysical modalities. She teaches at her center as well as schools and colleges throughout New England.

She has taught at the prestigious Lily Dale Assembly in Lily Dale, New York. One of Bonnie's passions is sharing her gift while demonstrating insight into the spirit world to audiences of all sizes. She presents in ballrooms, expos, fundraisers, and function facilities. Bonnie has two shows. Her LIVE Zoom Show "Who are you missing in Heaven"? can be found on her Facebook page MediumBonniePage. Her show "Ask The Psychic Medium" can be seen on Verizon and Comcast as well as YouTube.

Bonnie's Column "Ask the Psychic" can be found weekly in two papers in the New England Area and online. Her goal is to share her love of the spirit world with those here in the physical world, proving that our souls are eternal and live happily beside us every day.

Bonnie is happy to share her gift with others and feels inspired to do God's work by comforting those who need to hear from their loved ones on the other side. Her compassion, wisdom, and calming nature allows her clients to feel comfortable and at ease while receiving evidential proof that their departed loved ones are always close by and their soul is eternal.

For more information about Bonnie, please visit www.bonniepagemedium.com

CONTACT BONNIE PAGE:
Website: www.bonniepagemedium.com
Call or Email:
Phone: (978) 297-9790 (office)
Email: bonniepage@verizon.net
More Ways to Connect:
Facebook: www.facebook.com/MediumBonniePage
Instagram: Instagram.com/mediumbonniepage/